# There's Room for Everyone

## Accommodations, Supports, and Transitions— Infancy to Postsecondary

Isabel Killoran
and
Mark Brown, Editors

**Association for Childhood Education International**
17904 Georgia Ave., Ste. 215, Olney, MD 20832
www.acei.org • 800-423-3563

Bruce Herzig, ACEI Editor
Anne Bauer, ACEI Editor
Deborah Jordan Kravitz, Design and Production

Library of Congress Cataloging-in-Publication Data
There's room for everyone : accommodations, supports, and transitions - infancy
to postsecondary / Isabel Killoran and Mark Brown, editors.
    p. cm.
  Includes bibliographical references and index.
  ISBN-13: 978-0-87173-169-2 (pbk. : alk. paper)
  ISBN-10: 0-87173-169-X (pbk. : alk. paper)
  1.  Inclusive education--United States.  2.  Classroom management--United
States.  I. Killoran, Isabel. II. Brown, Mark.

LC1201.T47 2006
371.9'046--dc22
                                                              2006009548

# Table of Contents

# Introduction

**This** book differs from others because of its approach to inclusion, accommodations, and modifications. The authors start with the assumption that *all* children would be educated in their neighborhood community and in a general education classroom. They would have access to special educators who would collaborate with the general educator to include as much intervention as possible in that setting.[1] Some of you may come from areas where this is happening; others may only dream about it. Yet, we did not want to suggest that segregation is an acceptable option. If that option were included, many would be inclined to use it. Instead, we want you to read the chapters believing that inclusion is the norm; there should be no "Yeah, but," or "Everyone except. . . ." Inclusion is a right of all people.

We also included all educational levels. While most texts separate students by division, level, or ability, we see education/learning as an ongoing process. We wanted to provide the reader the opportunity to understand where the child may be coming from and where he or she might be going. We see disparate practices between divisions partly because of the lack of consideration of what type of environment and expectations a child had previously. Each state, province/territory, and/or country delineates education divisions using different criteria. Therefore, we have included applicable grades and ages as well as possible division names. Refer to the grade level if you are unsure of the correlation between division names used in this book and what you use.

We included the infant/toddler and preschool levels because of the incredible importance of creating a solid foundation for learning. It is during that critical stage when a child and her family gain a sense of whether or not they are accepted by the community. Preschool is the one level in which inclusion happens quite regularly, and the practice often can be maintained through kindergarten. As the child progresses through the levels, however, she is less likely to be included with her peers. Many will argue that this occurs because of the introduction of academic subjects and the child's inability to do them at the same level as her peers. We would argue that it is not the academic expectations that are the problem, but rather the expectations of the teacher regarding the child and academics. Once a teacher lets go of the belief that everyone needs to be at the same level, on the same page, in the same book, the classroom is freed up for all children.

We included the chapter on postsecondary education because children with disabilities will face three main roadblocks when they reach this level:

- The assumption that they cannot continue their education, when in fact many students with disabilities attend college, university, and apprenticeship programs.

- They "age out" of services and end up with nothing to do.
- They are not transitioned well into postsecondary education or employment opportunities.

Because of this last reason, we also have included a chapter on transitions. All children experience transition, whether they are small ones between activities or larger ones between schools. Some children with disabilities have an exceptionally difficult time with transition. Instead of having a little bit in every chapter about transition, we decided to dedicate a full chapter to this issue and thus bring to the topic the attention it deserves.

Without assistive technology (AT), many students would not be able to access the curriculum or demonstrate their learning. Consequently, the chapter on assistive technology is applicable to all levels, offering a broad look at both low-tech and high-tech accommodations. We provide many references to resources to help you as you begin to explore AT to make classrooms more accessible.

In creating the chapter format, we encouraged a vignette and case study. Problem-based learning is an effective way to apply what is read. Teachers often complain that they have not been told how to do something. It was not our goal to explain the "how," but rather to create a forum for discussion and reflection on practice. Each chapter can stand alone, which is what you may want if you are working with students or teacher candidates in a specific division. Or, the chapters can be read as if they were part of a developmental continuum, if you are teaching a course on inclusion or transitions. The vignettes at the beginning of each chapter set the stage for the classroom environment. The case study and questions following the chapter are specifically directed at the level or focus of the chapter.

We know that terminology is an issue in the field of special education, so we have tried to be as consistent as possible. We made sure that each chapter used the same terms, although they may be different from what you use. For example, in this book, an "accommodation" does not change the curriculum expectations, while a "modification" does. Most of what we have addressed here would be considered accommodations, although you can use these accommodations to deliver a modified program. "Adaptations" are defined as what is done or changed to make materials accessible. In order to fully appreciate the inclusiveness of the classrooms of which the authors write, you must approach them from the perspective of these definitions.

Finally, we would like to thank you for choosing to read this book. In doing so, you have moved closer to making inclusion a reality for all children.

**Note:**
[1] Services should be brought to children in their home school; however, there will be children who require a treatment program or intensive intervention (e.g., medical, psychological, behavioral) that cannot be carried out in the general education classroom or home school. These programs/interventions are only provided in extreme cases and often are not intended to be permanent. If a child needs to receive such service, the treatment plan should include beginning or returning to the home school as soon as possible, with follow-up service provided there.

# Chapter 1

# Why Inclusion?

*Isabel Killoran and Nancy Adams*

*Sunita anxiously waits for the bell to ring. It is recess time and she has to be the first one outside so she can claim the front wall for her friends. It's the best wall for playing Mother, May I?, their favorite game. Sunita maneuvers her motorized wheelchair to the front of the line beside Kristi. She whispers, "Don't worry, Kristi, I'll get to it first and save it for us." The bell rings and Sunita scoots into the hall, determined to beat the other grade 3 girls outside. Kristi stays right with her and pushes the automatic door opener so Sunita doesn't have to waste any time stopping to press it. She gets to the wall and her friends soon gather around and they begin to play. Sunita gets to be the mother first. After all, she was the one who saved the wall for them.*

A child's right to an education, which is entrenched in human rights declarations, has become a basic entitlement; however, granting a child's right to an education free from discrimination on the grounds of disability has not been widely practiced and has been formally (i.e., legally) recognized only in the last few decades. Some countries, such as Canada ("the first country to guarantee rights to people with disabilities in its Constitution"), have laws or charters that reference disability (Hutchinson, 2002, p. 5). For example, the *Canadian Charter of Rights and Freedoms* (Constitution Act, 1982) states that "every individual is equal before and under the law and has a right to the equal protection and equal benefit of the law without discrimination based on race, national or ethnic origin, colour, religion, sex, age, or mental or physical disability" (Section 15(1)).

Although many school districts and boards of education purport to be inclusive, the experiences of children with disabilities and their families indicate that true inclusion is not happening often enough. Many children are separated from their neighborhood friends to attend special education programs outside of their local community; others are placed in general education classrooms without the necessary supports[1] (Elementary Teachers' Federation of Ontario [ETFO], 2002). Some progress towards inclusion has been made, because various laws in North America require the consideration of the general education classroom before any other setting. We[2] have moved from the discourse of "if" inclusion is going to happen to one of "how" we can support it. The time has come to refuse any excuses and to demand the expectation that everyone is welcome in their community school.

In Ontario, we are in the process of closing the last of our residential institutions, yet can we honestly say that the communities to which the residents will return are prepared to embrace them, appreciate them, and include them in every way? Do the families and social agencies have the intention, motivation, and support needed to make this a successful transition? If our schools are to be used as the measuring stick of our commitment to inclusion, we cannot answer the questions in the affirmative. Although many education board representatives, administrators, and teachers live the philosophy of inclusion, many people still think that inclusion is optional. If, however, you believe that everyone, by virtue of being human, is entitled to the same human rights, there is no option.

"Inclusion" is a term that has been both misused and overused.[3] It is not a place, a program, or a curriculum. It's a way of thinking and a way of living. One cannot claim to be inclusive, yet find reasons to exclude children based on what they cannot do. Inclusion is a mindset—a belief in the value of each individual, a belief that everyone is a contributing member of society, and a conviction that our lives will be enriched by living this way.

For over 30 years, educators have been claiming not to have the funding, the resources, or the knowledge necessary to support inclusion (Bunch, Lupart, & Brown, 1997; Scruggs & Mastropieri, 1996). The personnel have changed, the curriculum has changed, and the children have changed, yet still we hear: "We are not equipped to accept children with special needs" and "We would not be able to work with an autistic child; there would be too many needs for that child" (Killoran, Tymon, & Frempong, in press).

No one claims that including everyone is easy or that school administrators and teachers won't have to spend additional time and effort creatively planning for the inclusion of all students. As advocates for students, teachers and support personnel need to put forth the necessary effort to successfully educate all children. When we asked teacher candidates why they chose the teaching profession, most responded that they did so "to make a difference." They didn't qualify their answer to extend that intention to only those who were typically able. What happens to these future teachers in their teacher preparation programs and during their first few years teaching that they begin to qualify their intent? How can faculties of education recruit, sustain, and support future teachers who admit that, despite their determination to make inclusion work, they don't always have the answer? An earlier study, of a cohort of elementary teacher candidates, showed a statistically significant decrease in positive attitudes towards inclusion, as measured from the beginning of their teacher preparation program to the end. Findings indicated that their faith in inclusion had lessened by the time they graduated (Killoran, 2000). Such results are unsettling and highlight the need for a discourse on rethinking education faculties' focus, the practicum experience, and the purpose of teacher preparation programs. Bratlinger (1997) suggests that "a basic requirement of any teacher education program should be to prepare preservice and inservice teachers to successfully include and engage diverse learners in inclusive classrooms" (p. 63). With this as a philosophical framework, faculties are more likely to graduate teachers who are supportive of, and prepared to teach in, inclusive classrooms.

We encourage faculties of education, as they rethink their programs, to consider the following three beliefs as a foundation to their educational framework and to prepare teacher candidates accordingly.

- Inclusion is a human rights issue.
- Segregation is discriminatory.
- Collaboration is central to success.

## Inclusion Is a Human Rights Issue

Several conventions and charters have granted children the right to an education. Their right not to be discriminated against because of disability is written into Canadian and American legislation, yet parents routinely have to fight for those services, accommodations, and modifications granted to their children under federal or local legislation[4]. If educators truly believed that disability was not a basis for exclusion, this discussion would not be necessary. Yet, Hansen (2001, as cited in Killoran, 2002), a retired superintendent of an inclusive Board of Education, identified statements often heard about those with disabilities:

"Disabled children have disruptive behaviours."
"Teachers should have the right not to work with students with disabilities."
"Disabled children should be with other disabled children." (p. 376)

We allow the above offensive statements regarding children with disabilities to go unchallenged, yet we would not allow the following statements:

"Blond children have disruptive behaviours."
"Teachers should not have to work with black children."
"Immigrant children, children of colour, aboriginal children should be with their own kind." (p. 376)

Many people still regard disability as a good enough reason to segregate children. Few equate discrimination based on disability with discrimination based on race or socioeconomic status. Consequently, negative attitudes toward inclusion, as represented in the above statements, are supported and even encouraged within the bureaucracy of schools.

When we are making comments and decisions about and for children with disabilities, we encourage reflection on the following questions:

* Is this how I would want to be treated?
* Would I want this for my child, my mother, my brother?
* Have I protected the dignity of the child?

Too often, decisions that will affect a child for the rest of his life are made hastily in 20-minute meetings (e.g., identification, placement, review committee meetings, or IEP meetings). We focus on assessments, test scores, what the child cannot do, and how difficult it is for the educator. We lose sight of the child—the human being with feelings, opinions, and rights.

## Segregation Is Discriminatory

We take children and try to fit them into our classrooms, our curriculum, and our belief systems. When they don't fit we discard them, arguing that they don't belong. We don't take responsibility for creating an environment that doesn't fit the child; instead, the onus is on the child to conform. We give up on them. We eloquently explain the many reasons why a child cannot be there; yet we offer no plans for what the child needs to do to be given access to the general education classroom. Once removed, it is almost impossible for a child to "earn" his way back into the general education setting. From a

**11**

traditional, medical perspective, this all makes sense. The child's diagnosis or identification is fact and will remain so. It is part of his biology. Under the medical model, the type of change needed to remove the label is not possible; therefore, the reason for exclusion will remain. Unless we change the paradigm under which we define disabilities and the people with them, we will not see the significant restructuring that is needed to make inclusion for all a reality.

Children who are segregated into self-contained settings do not do as well as children who are educated in inclusive settings (see, for example, Mason & Good, 1994; Oakes & Guiton, 1995; Rea, McLaughlin, & Walther-Thomas, 2002; Staub & Peck, 1995). Teachers' expectations in these settings are lower, and children live down to those expectations (Gartner & Lipsky, 1987; Linton, 1998). Eventually, the gap between what the child has learned in the segregated setting compared to what he would have learned in the general education setting becomes too large, or the child becomes too socially isolated, for a seamless re-entry. This is not to say that valuable work isn't being done with children in segregated settings—there absolutely is. The question is, why does it have to take place there? The following questions may help in planning:

- Can this activity be done with peers?
- How can the child's strengths be shared with others?
- What benefit is the child receiving in a segregated setting that could not be delivered in a general education classroom?

Of course, at times a child will need individualized services that require complete quiet or more physical space, such as speech and language therapy or orientation and mobility training. During these times, it may be necessary for the service provider to work with the child outside of the general education classroom. This should be done in such a way that it disrupts the child's time with his peers as minimally as possible, and the general education teacher should be part of the follow-up activities so it becomes part of the classroom routine. Regardless of the services a child receives, he is a part of the general education classroom and a responsibility of that educator. The services are brought to him and into the classroom whenever possible.

We cannot try to fit children into the systems we have now—systems that were designed for classrooms of homogeneous students. Current education sytems allow discrimination against children with disabilities to continue and prevent needed change from occurring (Bell, 1997; Bratlinger, 1997). Educators need to "make visible and vocalize the underlying assumptions that produce and reproduce structures of domination so that we can imagine alternative possibilities for organizing social life" (Freire, 1970; as cited in Bell, 1997, p. 11)[5]. What values do we hold that allow for the segregation of those with disabilities? What contributions do children with disabilities make in a general education classroom? What is a teacher's job? What is the ultimate goal of education? While examining these underlying assumptions, administrators at all levels need to rethink the distribution and use of funds and staff. Creatively grouping teaching teams, scheduling time for collaboration, and welcoming parental and community resources should form the foundation of the new plans. Administrators must decide that exclusion by disability cannot go on and will not be tolerated.

## Collaboration Is Critical for Success

Teachers have said for years that they cannot do their jobs alone, nor should they be expected to. Teachers are burning out and schools are experiencing high turnover, especially with new teachers (ETFO, 2002; Fore & Martin, n.d.; Ingersoll, 2001). Teachers need more support. To be fully effective, they need collaborative experiences with peers, parents, support personnel, and children (Meyen, Vergason, & Whelan, 1996; Pugach & Johnson, 1995). The value that North Americans place on independence has taken the focus away from collaboration and interdependence. We work in isolation, afraid to admit we do not know the answer, unwilling to risk asking for help. By its very nature, however, inclusion cannot work without collaboration. "In the absence of collaboration, it will be far more difficult to assure that all students not only are accepted in the schools but also are actively supported in accessing the full array of educational experiences" (Pugach & Johnson, 1995, p. 9).

Collaborative strategies, such as MAPS (Making Action Plans), PATH, and Circle of Friends, provide each person involved in a child's school experience (and beyond, at times) the opportunity to be heard and the ability to act (see Falvey, Forest, Pearpoint, & Rosenberg, 2000; Forest, Pearpoint, & O'Brien, 2000 for more information). When making decisions, we need to ask ourselves if we have listened to, valued, and incorporated the comments from parents, other staff members, community resource people, and, most important, the child.

Meeting children's diverse needs within the general education classroom can be challenging, but it is this very challenge that inspires inclusive practitioners. Upon the foundation of human rights, we create and support a community of learners—a community that appreciates each member, understands the importance of belonging, and works to make neighborhood schools accessible and welcoming for everyone. If you believe, as we do, that all humans are entitled to the same rights, then there is no other way to teach, to learn, or to live.

## Notes:

[1]Legislation in the United States, such as the No Child Left Behind Act, claims to address this type of issue.

[2]We have chosen to use "we" because we want all readers to be included in this discourse. Even advocates of inclusion, who work in inclusive settings, need to reflect on their practices, identify bias, and challenge themselves to provide an even better experience for children with disabilities.

[3]We purposely did not use the term "full inclusion" because we do not believe "partial inclusion" is an option.

[4]Education law is governed provincially/territorially in Canada. Each province and territory has its own legislation.

[5]Bratlinger (1997) provides beliefs that underpin inclusive and traditional schooling. It may be a good place to start if you are having difficulty identifying your beliefs about children with disabilities, the role of the teacher, and defining what education is and what it is for.

## References

Bell, L. (1997). Theoretical foundations for social justice education. In M. Adams, L. Bell, & P. Griffin (Eds.), *Teaching for diversity and social justice: A sourcebook* (pp. 3-15). New York: Routledge.

Bratlinger, E. (1997). Using ideology: Cases of nonrecognition of the politics of research and practice in special education. In S. Danforth & S. Taff (Eds.) (2003), *Crucial readings in special education* (pp. 56-75). Upper Saddle River, NJ: Prentice Hall.

Bunch, G., Lupart, J., & Brown, M. (1997). *Resistance and acceptance: Educator attitudes toward inclusion of students in regular classrooms.* Faculty of Education, York University, Toronto.

Constitution Act, 1982. *Schedule B, Part 1: Canadian Charter of rights and freedoms.* Retrieved on January 18, 2005, from http://laws.justice.gc.ca/en/charter/.

Elementary Teachers' Federation of Ontario (ETFO). (2002). *Fulfilling the promise: Ensuring success for students with special needs.* Toronto, ON: Author.

Falvey, M. A., Forest, M., Pearpoint, J., & Rosenberg, R. L. (2000). *All my life's a circle: Using the tools: Circles, MAPS & PATHS.* Toronto, ON: Inclusion Press.

Fore, C., III, & Martin, C. (n.d.). *Why do special education teachers leave the field? Possible methods to increase retention.* Retrieved on January 16, 2005, from www.hiceducation.org/Edu_Proceedings/Cecil%20Fore%20III.pdf.

Forest, M., Pearpoint, J., & O'Brien, J. (2000, July). Circle of friends: Not a program. *Inclusion News 2000,* p. 14.

Gartner, A., & Lipsky, D. K. (1987). Beyond special education: Toward a quality system for all students. In S. Danforth & S. Taff (Eds.) (2004), *Crucial readings in special education* (pp. 190-210). Upper Saddle River, NJ: Prentice Hall.

Hutchinson, N. (2002). *Inclusion of exceptional learners in Canadian schools.* Toronto, ON: Prentice Hall.

Ingersoll, R. M. (2001). *Teacher turnover, teacher shortages and the organization of schools.* Seattle, WA: University of Washington: Center for the Study of Teaching and Policy.

Killoran, I. (2000). *A longitudinal investigation of developmentally appropriate practice and inclusion perspectives held by prospective educators of young children.* Unpublished dissertation. Birmingham, AL: University of Alabama at Birmingham.

Killoran, I. (2002). A road less traveled: Creating a community where each belongs. *Childhood Education, 78,* 371-377.

Killoran, I., Tymon, D., & Frempong, G. (in press). Disabilities and inclusive practices within Toronto preschools. *International Journal for Inclusive Education.*

Linton, S. (1998). Divided society. In S. Danforth & S. Taff (Eds.) (2004), *Crucial readings in special education* (pp. 148-162). Upper Saddle River, NJ: Prentice Hall.

Mason, D., & Good, T. (1994). Effects of two-group and whole-class teaching on regrouped elementary students' mathematics achievement. *American Educational Research Journal, 30,* 328-360.

Meyen, E. L., Vergason, G. A., & Whelan, R. J. (1996). *Strategies for teaching exceptional children in inclusive settings.* Denver, CO: Love Publishing.

Oakes, J., & Guiton, G. (1995). Matchmaking: The dynamics of high school tracking decisions. *American Educational Research Journal, 32*(1), 3-33.

Pugach, M. C., & Johnson, L. J. (1995). *Collaborative practitioners, collaborative schools.* Denver, CO: Love Publishing.

Rea, P., McLaughlin, V., & Walther-Thomas, C. (2002). Outcomes for students with learning disabilities in inclusive and pullout program. *Exceptional Children, 68*(2), 203-222.

Scruggs, T. E., & Mastropieri, M. A. (1996). Teacher perceptions of mainstreaming/inclusion, 1958-1995: A research synthesis. *Exceptional Children, 63*(1), 59-74.

Staub, D., & Peck, C. (1994/95). What are the outcomes for nondisabled students? *Educational Leadership, 52*(4), 36-40.

## Case Study

*Sunita, age 8, belongs to a gregarious family. She lives with her parents, two brothers, a cat, a hamster, and a parakeet. She is the youngest and her dad and brothers often treat her like a baby. Her mother says it's only because of her disability, that they don't mean any harm by it. Nevertheless, it bothers Sunita, and she sometimes wonders if maybe they're right. Her mom encourages her to challenge their comments and prove to them that she can do anything they can do (not an easy task when one brother is a straight-A student and the other excels at track).*

*Sunita was born with spina bifida. She has a mild intellectual disability and usually uses a wheelchair to get around. Recently, she acquired a motorized one so she would find it easier to keep up with her family and friends. Sunita has been working with a physiotherapist and has good upper body strength. When she is at home, she often gets out of her wheelchair and plays on the floor. She is able to maneuver around the room to get whatever she needs. Sunita is very fortunate that her school is completely wheelchair accessible, but she sometimes feels funny sitting so much higher than her friends during assemblies and carpet time. Her best friend, Kristi, always sits on her knees beside her but that just makes both of them stick out.*

*Kristi comes over to her house to play most weekends, but Sunita has never been to Kristi's house, although they have been best friends since last year. Kristi's parents are afraid they won't know what to do if Sunita has to use the washroom or if she wants in or out of her chair. Besides, their house doesn't have a ramp. Kristi is having a slumber party for her 9th birthday. All the girls are invited, except Sunita. Kristi wants her to come, but her parents said, "No." Sunita is already dreading the Monday after the party. Everyone will be talking about the party at recess and she knows she will feel left out. She wonders if maybe her mom will let her stay home that day.*

## Questions

1. Can Sunita really do everything her brothers do? Is it right of her mother to say that she can?

2. Are Kristi's parents' concerns realistic? What can be done so Sunita can join in the birthday party? Or is it better if she doesn't go?

3. How can Sunita feel like she is part of the group during assemblies and carpet time?

4. If you were Sunita's parents, what would you need to do to address her inclusive issues with the school, with the teacher, with Kristi's parents?

# Chapter 2

# Infant-Toddler Years

*Patricia Hearron*

*Julius, a child with multiple, severe disabilities, including quadriplegic cerebral palsy and severe visual impairment, began attending a child development center with a mixed-age infant-toddler classroom at 16 months of age. From the beginning, his teacher, Elizabeth, made every effort to include Julius in what the other children were doing. For example, even before Julius could sit up at the table, Elizabeth made mealtimes a social occasion by pairing Julius with a younger child, Gavin, who had recently begun eating baby food. Rather than holding the boys individually and feeding them one at a time, Elizabeth propped them in side-by-side bouncy seats and sat facing them, chatting pleasantly as she spooned food from their individual dishes. Julius's mealtimes were punctuated by his shrill squeals of impatience when the next spoonful did not arrive quickly enough, but he became very quiet and listened attentively whenever Gavin chortled or babbled. Elizabeth was convinced that the two boys enjoyed their meals together.*

*Later that year, when Julius outgrew the bouncy seat but still needed to be supported in a sitting position, Elizabeth ordered a larger, sturdier model from a children's home-furnishings catalog. She left the package sitting in the toddler room for a few days, inviting the children to guess what was inside. (They inferred quite logically that there was a baby inside, since the carton was adorned with a picture of the seat occupied by a smiling child.) After three toddlers collaborated to open the carton (with Elizabeth's assistance), they all took turns sitting in Julius's new seat, just as they did a few months later when an adaptive chair was provided so Julius could sit at the lunch table with the other children. Often, when the physical therapist or vision specialist brought special toys or equipment to the classroom, their session with Julius became a small impromptu group activity.*

*Because the equipment, room arrangement, and staffing level made it easier to meet his physical needs, Julius remained in the infant-toddler room for one year after his age-mates moved into the preschool classroom. The mixed-age ranges in both classrooms meant that Julius still had friends among the younger children during that year, and when he did move, those who had gone on before him were still in the preschool classroom. Those age-mates remembered Julius well enough to show the teachers how singing "Twinkle, Twinkle, Little Star" calmed his squeals at group time. When the class was planning a parade to culminate their investigation of marching bands, it was the children who raised the question of how Julius could be included and then created the solution of working together to decorate his stroller.*

Including children with disabilities in programs serving infants and toddlers makes good sense for numerous reasons. For one thing, many of the needed resources, both material and human, are already in place. The physical environments of those programs are designed for, and equipped for the care of, babies who are at various stages of sitting up, walking, talking, or using the toilet independently, so it is not too great a stretch to care for children who acquire these skills more slowly (if at all) due to various types of disabilities. The skills that adults hone as they support typical development—careful observation, sensitivity, unobtrusive scaffolding—are equally or even more applicable when working with children whose development varies from typical patterns. The presence of typically developing peers can provide helpful models for children with disabilities to emulate, as well as a powerful motivating factor when their playful interactions are enjoyable. The return on the investment of those resources is further maximized because the learning goes both ways. For example, when 15-month-old Angela enrolled in an infant-toddler program, her tracheotomy hindered her vocal expression and she was learning some basic sign language. Soon, all the children in the program were signing "more" and "all done" at the lunch table or "change" as they toddled toward the diapering table. The vignette at the beginning of this chapter demonstrates what is perhaps an even more important benefit: When adults support their budding relationships, children without disabilities learn empathy and helpfulness; they learn not to ignore differences, but to see beyond them.

Inclusion in infant-toddler programs is thus the first step toward lifelong inclusion as members of a community. Such programs are not limited to group care facilities; in fact, group settings may be inadvisable for children whose biological risk factors heighten their susceptibility to infection (Guralnick, 2000, p. 227). Many children, with or without disabilities, spend the first few years of their lives at home with their families. This may be a matter of preference, as in countries where family welfare policies include paid parental leave, or a matter of necessity, as in countries where care for infants and toddlers is in short supply and high-quality care almost nonexistent. Inclusion means that children with disabilities have access to the same experiences and opportunities as their peers without disabilities, and that they receive the support necessary to participate in and benefit from those experiences. Neighborhood play groups, "mom and tot" groups that meet once a week, and classes such as "baby gymboree" are all potentially inclusive settings for infants and toddlers, given the appropriate adaptations and accommodations. Some countries have introduced legislation to identify children with disabilities as early as possible so that they can receive early intervention. The United States has introduced the individualized family service plan (IFSP) as the framework for intervention for children ages birth to 3, as a reflection of the importance of tailoring services for very young children to family needs and dynamics. Unlike the individualized education plan (IEP) for older children, which focuses on a child's functioning in school, the IFSP addresses family needs and concerns and typically includes a range of goals and strategies to be carried out in a variety of settings. While this chapter focuses primarily on group care settings, the basic principles and strategies discussed apply wherever children are served.

## Starting With the Basics

In our eagerness to help a child compensate for disabilities and to reach particular milestones, it is sometimes easy to forget to focus on the child first, then on the disability. But *all* children share basic needs for safe, sanitary, and healthful environments; for relationships with caring and responsive adults to promote a sense of security; and for opportunities to explore, understand, and control their environment (Cryer, 2000). A detailed discussion of recommended health and sanitation practices is beyond the scope of this chapter. Readers are encouraged to consult with local public health or licensing authorities for specific guidance.

Emotional security, which is closely related to concepts of attachment and trust, is the foundation upon which all other types of development are built. Before any child can take in new sensations or move out to explore her environment, she needs to feel reasonably calm and alert. This feeling comes partly as a consequence of physical comfort: the sensations of warm, dry clothing on clean skin and a pleasantly full tummy; having peace and quiet, but not too much; having the stimulation of interesting things to see, hear, touch, and do, but not too much. Deciding how much is "enough" and how much is "too much" will require careful observation and sensitivity to the child's cues. Children with limited or no vision, for example, seem to feel more secure when they are placed in relatively confined spaces where they can use boundaries to orient themselves.

Physical comfort is not enough, however; nor is it possible to maintain this perfect state forever. Hunger and dirty diapers are recurring facts of life. In order to cope with occasional discomfort, *all* babies need the emotional or psychological comfort of knowing that they can expect things to get better when they feel cold, wet, or hungry. Furthermore, they need to learn that they have a role in making that happen. This means that the *way* in which they are fed or changed is just as important—perhaps even more important—as simply meeting these physical needs. When the same person (or two or three people) consistently provide those warm, loving interactions, babies (as well as their caregivers) develop feelings of connectedness called "attachment." The role of the caregiver is important, but babies are hardly passive partners in the attachment process. Bowlby (1989) argues that babies have an entire repertoire of behaviors (like crying, clinging, cooing, and smiling) that seem almost guaranteed to bring out the kinds of responses they need from their caregivers. As infants get older and more mobile, they are able to take an even more active role in staying close to the important people in their lives; they follow them around, first on all fours and then on two feet. Various types of disabilities can interfere with this process if infants do not cling, vocalize, or smile, or if they lack the mobility to follow their caregivers. Therefore, adults need to observe closely and respond to subtle signs that children are reaching out to them. Secure attachment affects later psychological development and coping ability (Ainsworth, 1967; Gunnar, 1996; Stroufe, 1995), and there is no reason to think that these long-term consequences do not hold equally true for children with disabilities.

For all these reasons, then, your first order of business with any child is to form a relationship that will help that child feel secure. Relationships start with getting to know each other, and this applies to relationships with babies as well. How does LaToyah like to be held when she is fed? Does she seem to enjoy a soft touch on her skin during diapering, or does it seem to irritate her and make her squirm away? Does she wake up hungry and go from a sound sleep to red-faced screaming panic in a matter of seconds? Or does she lie in her crib and gaze quietly at the mobile until you notice she is awake? When a sudden loud noise happens to startle her awake, can she calm herself back to sleep or does she need to be cuddled and soothed? When you know these things about LaToyah, you are able to read her signals and meet her needs more effectively. Consequently, she spends less time feeling that no one understands her, and gradually develops the confidence that she can make her needs known and that help will come.

When meeting a new child, particularly a child with a disability, you might feel overwhelmed by the need to learn all this. But rest assured, you have a powerful teacher and ally in the baby herself. In many cases, if you listen and watch carefully, she will tell you what she needs. Certainly, crying is one way that babies communicate their needs, and babies have a wide repertoire of other tools for communication as well. Babies typically gaze intently into your face, follow the sound of your voice, and even imitate your expressions or sounds. They yawn or turn their faces aside when incoming sensations are overwhelming. Their skin reddens, or they squirm and flail their limbs when they are upset. They vocalize and kick or wave their arms when they are enjoying your attention. Their faces crumple and they begin to drool when wanted attention is withheld. They cuddle into your arms when they want to be held or stiffen themselves when they don't. A particular disability might preclude use of one or more means of expression, but that is all the more reason for adults to be sensitive to other signals.

Luckily, babies, including those with disabilities, make good teachers for another reason besides their mastery of such a wide "vocabulary." They also happen to be quite forgiving of mistakes and persistent in trying to help you get it right. Dr. Berry Brazelton, a renowned pediatrician who has helped countless parents become more sensitive observers of their children, tells anxious new parents that the only way to learn to be a parent is to make mistakes. The same comforting advice applies to the other adults in a baby's life. The trick is to ask babies what they want of you, or to tell them what you intend to do with them, then wait a moment or two for a response or signal from them before proceeding. The baby lying quietly on a blanket who begins to squirm and vocalize may merely want a little conversation and human contact. A sensitive caregiver moves close, speaks the baby's name, perhaps asking, "Are you ready to be picked up, LaToyah?" and then waits a few seconds for LaToyah's response before picking her up. Depending on the nature of a child's disability, it may be necessary to wait longer for a response. Perhaps LaToyah stops squirming and her face takes on an intent look of concentration, as though she were mulling over the prospect. Perhaps she turns her gaze toward the sound of your voice, or makes a cooing sound that echoes your intonation. Whatever form her response takes, waiting for it gives her a chance to process what she has heard, to focus her attention, and to prepare for what happens next.

Once you pick her up, allowing for another pause, perhaps giving LaToyah a chance to gaze at your face or at the world over your shoulder, will tell you whether she is satisfied with the change of scenery or she wants something else. And so the cycle continues, with you observing LaToyah and fine-tuning your actions in response to her signals. In contrast to this subtle "dance," swooping LaToyah into your lap and plopping a bottle in her mouth, without confirming that she is indeed hungry, will lead to frustration for both of you. This practice of observing, waiting, and giving cues that help babies prepare themselves for what happens next are part of what Magda Gerber (1998) advocates as responsive and respectful caring. In essence, the strategies for smoothing a first encounter with any child are simple courtesies that will help lay the foundation for a good relationship with a child who happens to have a disability.

The benefits of primary caregiver relationships that are maintained through the child's first three years of life are doubly important for children whose disabilities may make it more challenging for them to forge connections. As they interact with each other day after day, both child and caregiver become more skillful at anticipating, communicating, and responding to each other's actions. Family members are likely to feel more comfortable coming to a primary caregiver when they have a question or concern if they can usually count on that person to know enough about their child to answer their questions and understand their concerns.

Unfortunately, many babies in group care settings experience a disruption in their lives every few months as they are "moved up" to the next age group to make room for new arrivals. Even in very high-quality programs, ones with a particular focus on sustained relationships, only about half the children have formed secure attachments after six months with the same caregiver. After nine months, about two thirds of the children are securely attached, and 91 percent by one year (Raikes, 1996). These statistics suggest that children who are routinely moved to the "next" group at six-month intervals may never form a secure attachment with a caregiver. According to Lally and his colleagues, "When a very young child loses a caregiver, he loses part of his sense of himself and of how the world operates" (Lally et al., 1995, p. 34). All the hard work of figuring out each other's signals must begin again for the child, for the caregiver, and for family members, with inevitable frustration and stress on all sides. If this is true for children with typical development, think of how much more discouraging it must be for children whose disabilities mean that they and their caregivers have to work even harder to become comfortable with each other. When this happens over and over, babies can give up and stop trying to connect with their new caregivers. Ironically, their aloofness might be interpreted as adjusting well to the changes! Another consequence, seldom considered, is the loss of relationships between children, which, although barely formed, nevertheless exist, as seen so vividly in the vignette at the beginning of this chapter.

## Transdisciplinary Approach

The importance of security and attachment makes a powerful argument for adopting a transdisciplinary approach to providing services for babies with disabilities. It is not unusual for a child with disabilities to be seen and treated by a number of different specialists. A physical therapist might carry out positioning exercises one day; a vision specialist might visit the next day with a collection of toys to elicit tracking; a nutritionist might be involved to work on feeding and swallowing issues; and a speech-language pathologist might work with the child's articulation. It is hard for a baby with typical development to adjust to new faces. Imagine the added challenge for a child who cannot see those faces clearly and who adjusts to any new experience more slowly. In the transdisciplinary approach, professionals and parents work as a team to plan the best way to meet the child's needs and, where possible, designate the person most familiar to the child and family to carry out specific activities or interventions, based on directions and consultation from the various specialists. This not only reduces the child's stress of coping with so many different people, but also increases the likelihood that the intervention strategies will become part of the child's daily routine.

In an ideal world, those specialists would spend time talking to the primary caregiver and observing the child in the group setting before entering the scene to conduct assessments or provide therapies. They would acquire a more comprehensive and accurate picture of both the child's abilities and the ways the program is already fostering those abilities. Armed with this knowledge, they then could identify potential accommodations or adaptations that would enhance the child's experiences without placing undue burdens on caregivers. And they would teach those techniques to caregivers so that the desired skills could be addressed more frequently and in more naturalistic contexts. For example, a speech therapist who wants to encourage a child to ask, rather than just sign, for "more," could suggest that caregivers serve snacks in smaller portions and encourage a verbal request before providing seconds. The specialists' crowded schedules as well as funding policies biased toward a direct service model (as opposed to a consultative model) make it harder to achieve a truly transdisciplinary approach; nevertheless, it is a worthy goal.

### Moving From Security to Exploration

After children get to know you and begin to feel comfortable in your care, you continue to foster security in the following ways:

• Meet the child's physical needs as promptly as possible. This means being sensitive to children's signals that they are hungry or tired and being sufficiently organized to respond quickly. It means anticipating those needs so that lunch is served before children are too tired and hungry to eat it. The more you are able to give children what they need and when they need it, the more they will come to trust you. Of course, a child may need something while your hands are full with another. If you have been a reliable source of comfort in the past, you can help a child endure a short wait by telling her what you are doing and that you are coming right away.

• Touch and hold each child frequently. Babies—with or without disabilities—need to be held. They do not need motorized bouncy seats, automatic swings, or vibrating crib pads. They need human touch. Here again, however, the importance of sensitive observation cannot be overstated. Babies should not be treated like inanimate cuddly toys, to be picked up and squeezed on a whim. They need some way to anticipate your touch, and you need to watch for signs that tell you whether or not they are enjoying it. For the child who cannot see you, it means speaking gently before touching; for the child who cannot hear, it might mean moving into his or her line of vision. Discovering the particular ways that each baby likes to be touched can be an intriguing and pleasant part of your job.

• Lift and hold babies appropriately. When lifting babies whose neck muscles lack the strength to support their heads (whether newborns or children with disabilities like cerebral palsy), be sure that one hand is securely positioned beneath the head and neck, with the other hand beneath the buttocks. When holding a baby upright, with his head resting on your shoulder, again make sure that you firmly support the baby's head and spine with one hand and the buttocks with the other. Many babies feel more secure when they are swaddled; that is, when they are wrapped snugly in a lightweight blanket so that their limbs are held close to their bodies. Swaddling is especially effective in soothing babies who have been exposed to drugs during their prenatal development. Another helpful technique with these babies is vertical rocking—holding a swaddled baby with her feet aimed toward your body so that the baby's head is lifted and lowered as you rock back and forth. As always, you must carefully support the baby's head, neck, and spine with your hands and arms.

• Provide a secure base for babies who can move about. Sit where they can easily come back to you between forays. Make frequent eye contact (or voice contact for children with limited vision) and speak to them as they go about their explorations. Try to stay put as long as possible, and when you do have to move away or out of sight, tell them where you are going and come back as quickly as possible.

• Develop comforting, playful rituals with individual children. Your life with infants and toddlers is full of small events that are repeated every day or many times each day. These events become rituals when they are repeated in the same way each time; when they raise a child's expectations that something will happen, immediately fulfill those expectations. Carrying a baby to the window to let him wave good-bye to his family member before he goes off to play each morning is a ritual. Rituals promote security because they are predictable and help babies (as well as adults) manage many aspects of life. If you melodiously recite, "One, two, three . . . upsa-daisy," each time you lift a child to the diapering table, you will know you have established a ritual when that child smiles and lifts her arms expectantly, perhaps even chiming in, as soon as you begin to count.

## Providing Stability

Stability for babies means predictability. Babies should have their own cribs or cots and their own spaces in which to store their personal belongings. Family members should know where these places are located. The length of activities should be predictable, but the boundaries between events should be fluid and overlapping. The rhythm of the daily schedule should be associated with a predictable setting for each part of that schedule. That way, regardless of which sense modality they use most efficiently, children learn a variety of cues that help them predict what will happen next. A hungry baby might recognize the sensation of being held and rocked a particular way as meaning that a warm bottle is on the way. Once babies become mobile and develop longer memories, security can come from knowing that a favorite toy or cozy nook will be where it was the day before.

Babies gain a sense of stability when they find that the world is a predictable place, that they are safe and welcome, and that their feelings and interests matter; stability also means freedom from overstimulation or jarring sensory experiences. Unfortunately, many child care centers are modeled after schools and use harsh, fluorescent lighting, which creates an institutional atmosphere that does not promote the sensation of security and home. The effect is compounded for the youngest babies, who spend so much of their day lying down and looking up at the ceiling. More soothing alternatives are filtered natural light, fixtures that create pools of light in particular areas, or track lighting, which can be diffused by bouncing it off walls. The ideal auditory environment is relaxing and quiet enough that children and adults can hear each other. It might include the sound of breezes and birdsongs outside the window. Unavoidable intrusive noises from an urban environment might be masked with white noise from a fan. Constant "background" music, such as that from a radio or television, is distracting and eventually trains children to tune out the sounds in their environment; it is especially detrimental for individuals with hearing impairments. The olfactory environment can enhance or detract from children's experiences and the overall quality of life for everyone in the facility. Again, the ideal is fresh air from open windows and the fresh scent of clean laundry, as opposed to stale air or either the odor of dirty diapers or the chemicals used to mask it. Pleasant aromas of bread baking or aromatic herbs add interest, but it is important to avoid perfumes and artificially scented lotions that can cause reactions in sensitive children.

## Exploration

Once babies feel secure, they can reach out to explore their world. That exploration is the way that babies learn. Your job, after making sure that each baby feels safe and comfortable, emotionally as well as physically, is to support that exploration. Sometimes you accomplish both aims at once. For example, when you pick up a crying baby, your intention might be to soothe and comfort, to provide reassurance that the world will respond to his needs. In the process, however, the baby's brain forms a neural pathway, a connection between the act of crying and the relief of tension that comes when you pick him up. He *learns* that he can have an effect on his world. Listening and responding to the rhythm and intonation of your voice lays an important foundation for later language development. Furthermore, from his new upright position, he can look over your shoulder at an entire world that he could not see while lying on his back in the crib; he has a new visual environment to explore. Thus, you moved from promoting security to supporting exploration within the framework of a single interaction.

Did you accomplish the first aim and then move to the second? Perhaps, but it might be more accurate to say that, by the time the baby was gazing contentedly over your shoulder, you were actually doing both at once. Establishing security had to happen first, though. If the baby had continued crying after being picked up, he would have been much less likely to take a spontaneous interest in his new view, and even less likely to participate in any "learning activity" you might have planned. Infant-toddler professionals need to be able to do many things at once, and they need to know when to shift emphasis from one goal to another. Luckily, the babies themselves will be powerful allies in accomplishing this feat, and the point—as always—is to take your cues from them.

## Support vs. Stimulation

You may have heard people say that babies need stimulation in order to develop and learn. It is more accurate to say that they need the right amount of stimulation, neither too much nor too little, and they need it at the right time. Unfortunately, the concept of stimulation can be misinterpreted to mean that babies are passive creatures who would never learn anything without conscious adult intervention. Misguided "infant-stimulation" programs ask adults to do things *to* babies, to get babies to perform. They might suggest, for example, that caregivers clap or click their fingers or move a brightly colored object across the baby's field of vision, to see if the baby will turn his head toward the sound or track the moving object with his eyes.

There is nothing inherently wrong or harmful about these activities in themselves. They may, in fact, be useful strategies for professionals responsible for assessing or ameliorating a child's functioning in a particular area. The problem occurs when untrained adults impose these activities on children as though "stimulation" were a commodity that could be distributed in prescribed doses, like chewable vitamins. It is easy for adults to become so focused on their own agenda of providing adequate stimulation that they fail to take into account the fact that babies have an agenda, too: they want to make sense of their world. They are active participants in their own learning and development, full of their own questions and ideas about how the world works. What they need, then, is support for their efforts, not prepackaged bits of stimulation. This view corresponds with constructivist theories of development, particularly that of Piaget, as well as with Magda Gerber's (1998) concept of respectful caregiving.

Your careful observation and sensitive responses will help you provide what each baby needs when he or she needs it. Perhaps you move close to where 2-month-old Dante is lying on a blanket on the floor. As he moves his arms and legs, his feet accidentally push against your hand. He smiles, gurgles, and begins to move more vigorously, apparently enjoying the sensation of pressure on his feet. You accept his invitation and begin a gentle game of letting him push against your hand, moving it away, and bringing it back.

## Importance of Play

Brain research tells us that each movement, sensation, or discovery has the potential to form connections within the baby's brain. These connections, which literally change the brain's structure, are less likely to occur when babies are distressed. Absence of distress only sets the stage, however. New connections are most likely to occur when babies are engaged in interesting, pleasurable activities—when they play. Play seems to be nature's way of continuing the brain construction process that begins before birth. Through play, babies discover new abilities and refine those abilities with practice. They combine abilities to make other new discoveries, and the cycle of exploration and mastery begins anew. As they play, babies learn about the people and objects around them, and they learn the many ways they can affect those people and objects. Play is so crucial for a child's development that much of your day will be devoted to observing, supporting, and enriching it.

Linder (1993) found several key differences in the play of children with disabilities: it is often less organized and more ritualistic, involving less language and less pretending. Children with disabilities are more likely to play alone than in groups and might not be chosen as play partners by other children. Play is the primary means by which children learn, however, and the development of children whose play is limited as a result of their disabilities is further impeded when this path is inaccessible to them. To make matters worse, programs for children with disabilities often tend to undervalue the intrinsic value of play, and their administrators view play as a vehicle for promoting educational or therapeutic goals. Unfortunately, this approach loses sight of the fact that children are functioning at their highest levels when they truly play—when they are fully engaged, exuberant, mischievous, and joyful. For children with disabilities, genuine play can help reduce feelings of learned helplessness, but none of these benefits can occur unless adults support play for ALL children (http://letsplay.buffalo.edu/products/presentations.htm).

## Types of Play

Babies play in several ways:

- They play at first with their own fingers, toes, voices, and sensory experiences.
- They play with objects.
- They play with movement.
- They play with other people.
- They play with language.

As you observe the children in your care from week to week and month to month, you will notice that each of these types of play changes with time. Pure sensorimotor play disappears as the other types of play become more complex. You will also notice that these categories are somewhat arbitrary, and that they overlap in many instances. The following section examines the types of play as well as the ways that you can support that play.

**Sensorimotor Play**

In the earliest months of life, the baby seems to ask, "What can I do?" His gaze falls upon a sunbeam dancing on the wall next to his crib or upon your face as you hold him in your arms. He looks and keeps on looking, prolonging the enjoyment. He kicks and thrusts his arms several times, apparently for the pure pleasure of the movement. After a few months, his attention turns from the sensations within his own body to the objects around him and he begins to discover connections between the two, at first accidentally and later more purposefully. The mobile over his crib might jiggle when he kicks or someone might talk back when he coos, so he continues these activities to extend these intriguing phenomena. With increasing dexterity, and more experience with cause and effect, his actions will become more intentional. Instead of waiting for things to happen as a result of his random activity, he will begin to make them happen. He begins to ask, "What does this do? What can I do with it? What happens if I do this?"

Young infants, or any children unable to move independently, need help if they are to explore interesting aspects of their world. Keep in mind that babies might find interesting many things that seem rather mundane to you. After all, their experience of life on this planet is much more limited than yours. This means that simple, everyday items can fill the bill just as well as expensive toys can. Also remember that the most interesting "thing" you can bring to the baby is yourself. Babies prefer to look at things with sharp contrasts, especially eyes, and things that make gratifying noises or movements in response to some action of theirs. You fill all those requirements much better than the most sophisticated toy. In other words, toys are supplements, not substitutes for interaction with you.

With this caveat in mind, you can, nevertheless, support and extend sensorimotor play with thoughtfully selected toys and materials. For all children, and particularly for children whose disability limits their use of one or more senses, it is important to match toy characteristics to the child's abilities and preferences. Appeal to the sense of sight with toys that have interesting shapes, shiny surfaces or mirrors, or those that move (e.g., mobiles). For children who respond more readily to sound, try toys that make music or noise or simple household items like metal spoons or keys. Soft toys, knobby balls, vibrating toys, crinkly newspaper, and wet or dry washcloths all appeal to the sense of touch. Remember that children, even those who prefer or have limited use of one sensory modality, display individual differences in range of ability as well as personal preference.

A word of caution is in order here. Some adults, including caregivers with responsibility for too many children at one time, sometimes use toys and equipment as tools for lulling babies, if not to sleep, at least to quietness. In some centers, babies are picked up from their cribs, fed and diapered, and plopped in automatic swings, which caregivers crank up again whenever the babies squirm or make a sound. Children with disabilities are similarly "parked" in between sessions with their various therapists. Apart from the harm that slouching in the swing can do to a baby's developing spine, this perpetual maintenance of a semi-hypnotic state directly contradicts the goal of high-quality care, which is to support the kinds of exploration that help babies grow and learn. Certainly, soothing fussy babies is a legitimate goal. We know that babies have a harder time taking in information when they are upset; however, drowsy babies are at a similar disadvantage. In between fussing and drowsiness is the quiet alert state during which babies are primed for absorbing and processing sensory experiences. Using play materials to induce or to take advantage of the quiet alert state should not be confused with using them to keep babies quiet.

Nevertheless, even the most well-attended babies spend some waking moments or "down time" in their cribs, perhaps as they settle down to sleep, perhaps while their caregivers are occupied with other children. They take in information during those moments just as they do at other times, and for that reason, it can be worthwhile to provide some simple crib accessories that invite exploration and arouse curiosity. Mobiles, particularly those that that move gently or play soft music, can provide some relief to the monotony of staring at the blank ceiling. Older babies will prefer those that they can make move by kicking or batting, and eventually they will want to touch and manipulate the parts of the mobile. Mobiles that are too fragile to withstand this kind of use must be removed from cribs or raised out of reach before children are able to grasp the pieces. They can be replaced with crib gyms for children with disabilities who prefer playing while lying on their back, and will benefit from such adaptations as attachments that lower the suspended toys to bring them within the child's reach, thus encouraging and supporting their exploration. Bells fastened to babies' ankles jingle pleasantly when they kick, and help babies discover connections between their actions and the subsequent sound. Some babies will prefer to play while lying on their side or on their tummy, but will need support so they can direct their energy to playing rather than maintaining their position. Cushions, stuffed animals, commercial props, or your lap can all serve this purpose.

No matter how well-furnished the crib, its value as support for exploration is limited. In addition to time in your arms, babies need daily time on blankets on the floor, where they can see more and have a greater range of movement. When one or two other babies are nearby on the floor, the possibilities for exploration are multiplied. Babies are always intrigued by other babies, although your support will be needed to help them investigate without offending or hurting each other.

Taking the baby to see and hear interesting things can be as simple as carrying him with you as you walk across the room to enter feeding and diapering records on a wall chart. In that case, the journey is more important than the destination. The new view of the room over your shoulder, and your commentary on what the baby sees, will transform this mundane chore into a small adventure for the baby. A little further afield, going outdoors provides a feast of sensory experiences. Birds flit across the sky; leaves rustle in the wind; the scent of newly mown grass or rain-dampened earth fills the nostrils; cool breezes and warm sunshine caress the skin. Note that babies' tender skin is particularly vulnerable to sunburn and must be protected by lightweight clothing, sunscreen (although the use of sunscreen is not recommended before 6 months of age), and shade. It also makes sense to avoid the hours immediately before and after noon, when sunlight is most intense.

## Play With Objects

Gradually, babies' interest shifts from focusing on their own physical sensations to exploring and acting on the objects around them. Well-chosen toys encourage babies to investigate and form hypotheses about their world. As they play, some of the questions they consider and discover the answer to include: "If this rattle makes such an intriguing sound when I shake it, will this teether do the same thing? Will it squeak if I bite it? Or rattle if I shake it? Can I squeeze this rattle?" Eventually, when they begin to dump these toys out of the tubs or pails where they are stored, babies will form concepts such as "empty," "full," "in," "out," and "all gone."

For safety's sake, all these toys must be sturdy, made of non-toxic material, and free of small parts that can choke a child should they become dislodged and swallowed. For young infants, or for children with limited muscle control, it can be helpful to contain some toys in trays with raised edges or to fasten them to a tabletop with suction cups or to wristbands with Velcro. That gives the child an opportunity to explore the toy without the frustration of inadvertently knocking it out of reach. It is important to provide children with toys for which they have the needed strength and range of motion and to avoid toys that overwhelm children with too many bells and whistles. The best toys are the ones that can be used in different ways as children grow or change positions.

Babies' tastes in toys change as they become able to sit up and use both hands in a more or less coordinated way. Instead of toys that are simply mouthed or banged, they want toys they can manipulate, like pop-beads, keys on rings, balls, and simple blocks. Sturdy puzzles with knobs and no more than 2 or 3 pieces are appealing, as are toys like stacking rings, which are really three-dimensional puzzles. Again, these toys need not be expensive or even purchased. Babies will be just as happy—and learn just as much—from playing with homemade equivalents. Instead of ordering the expensive nesting toys from a catalog, you might ask families to help you collect clean, safe household items, such as plastic measuring cups or food storage containers to stack, or wooden clothespins to drop in (and dump out of) a wide-mouthed plastic juice bottle. Think of all the things a baby can do with an empty stainless steel mixing bowl: pick it up, drop or toss it, bang it on the floor, chew on its edge, turn it over and bang on it, fill it with smaller objects that make satisfying clinking sounds, dump it out and start over, hide behind it for peek-a-boo, gaze at the changing patterns reflected on its shiny surface, or wear it like a hat and giggle at the joke.

As babies gain experience and skill, they begin to use objects in more complex ways. Often, this complexity takes the form of incorporating objects into other types of play, such as motor play or pretend play, which will be discussed later. But babies also love to explore new uses for objects, and enjoy combining them with other materials. Instead of just carrying or kicking a ball, they might drop it on a ramp and watch it roll down. Instead of just making a switch-operated toy stop and go, a child can make it knock down a block structure or race with another child's toy. The measuring cups that have been chewed, banged, and stacked inside each other acquire new life as vessels for pouring and filling with sand or water. Adults support this developing complexity by providing the ramp, the blocks to knock down, or the sand or water when observation suggests that babies are ready for this type of play.

## EQUIPMENT FOR SUPPORTING
## EXPLORATION WITH HANDS AND ARMS

| Grasping | • Textured balls<br>• Toys and puzzle pieces with small knobs<br>• Fluffers or tabs on book pages to make turning them easier |
|---|---|
| Striking | • Sturdy, securely fastened objects suspended within arm's reach of baby<br>• Lightweight bats or paddles that toddlers can use to strike suspended, soft balls<br>• Balls that light up or make sounds |
| Throwing | • Lightweight balls of various sizes, including large beach balls<br>• Beanbags (securely closed to prevent accidental swallowing of contents)<br>• Baskets, buckets, or boxes to throw things into |
| Scribbling | • Large paper taped to table or wall<br>• Brushes with knobby handles<br>• Foam padding around markers or crayons for easier gripping |

## Variety and Organization

Play materials are the tools with which children build their knowledge and skills, and it takes thoughtful effort to make these tools available in the ways that will be most useful to children. As noted above, because babies differ in their abilities and preferences, you need to provide a variety of different types of materials. Too many choices, on the other hand, can be as detrimental to play as too few choices. Babies might be unable to choose, or even unable to see their choices, if they are overwhelmed with too many possibilities. Consequently, they might play with one particular toy in repetitive and stereotyped ways, or they might wander among the possibilities, dumping things out, but never going any further in their explorations.

Faced with too many possibilities, children may begin to disregard the materials that remain day in, day out. By rotating the toy selection, caregivers are acknowledging that babies change over time and that their own new skills will enable them to see old materials with new eyes after a brief absence. At the same time, babies need predictability and stability in their environments as much as they need novelty. There can be no standard prescription for striking just the right balance between these two qualities. If you observe carefully, you will notice when babies seem to tire of certain materials and you will have some idea of what individual babies like to do, which can guide your choice of what to make available next.

## Play With Movement

Adults support children's enjoyment of physical activity by providing opportunities for safe movement, and encouraging children when they make use of those opportunities. This support is essential if babies are to use and develop their motor skills and can take many forms:

• Give babies opportunities to experience a variety of positions throughout the day, such as when they are picked up, held, rocked, fed, and diapered. Research in institutional settings demonstrates that when babies are not held and handled in these ways, their physical development is delayed (Keogh & Sugden, 1985, p. 381).

- Give babies opportunities to do the things they already can do in different places. While lying on their backs on the floor, babies see things from a different angle and feel different textures on their skin; also, the harder floor provides more resistance than their crib mattresses when they push against it to roll over.
- Notice and talk to babies about what they are doing; cheer their accomplishments and encourage them in their struggles.
- Give babies time to solve their own problems before jumping in to rescue them, thereby supporting cognitive and emotional, as well as physical, development.
- Supervise carefully so that babies cannot hurt themselves or others.
- Provide toys and spaces that tempt babies to use and enjoy their emerging skills.

### PRINCIPLES FOR ARRANGING TODDLER PLAY SPACES

| Principle | Examples | Accommodations or Modification |
|---|---|---|
| Provide defined spaces for each type of activity | • Soft area in which children and adult can snuggle with books<br>• Enclosed area for stacking blocks, or filling and dumping them without interference<br>• "Messy" area with washable floor and nearby water supply for painting and water or sand play | • Entrance to each area is wide enough to accommodate children in standers<br>• Take children to areas they cannot access on their own, observe carefully and respond when they are ready to move away from an area |
| Create zones for types of play, using low barriers that allow for visual supervision from any point in the room | • Separate areas for quiet activities and for more boisterous activities<br>• Protected areas for blocks and construction; puzzles and manipulatives; dress-up and dramatic play; art; sand and water; books<br>• Open space in middle for gross motor activity | • Place materials in each area on levels each child can access (e.g., locks on raised platforms for children in standers)<br>• Encourage play involving children with and without disabilities; supervise carefully |
| Use boundaries to distinguish zones | • Low shelving<br>• Carpeted vs. tiled floor surface<br>• Risers<br>• Platforms, lofts<br>• Curtains | For children with limited vision:<br>• very high contrast or tactile boundaries<br>• keep room arrangement consistent over time |
| Organize materials and furnishings within each area | • Store items near location of their intended use (e.g., puzzles on low shelves near table or floor area earmarked for manipulatives)<br>• Help children become aware of organization (place like items near each other on shelves, with plenty of space around each; transparent bins so children can see small items stored inside) | Store adaptive supplies as needed in each area<br>• Short lengths of foam pipe insulation to slip over knobs on puzzle pieces, making them easier to grasp<br>• Tape-recorded narrations of picture- and storybooks for children with vision impairment |

*(Based on Lally et al., 1995; Torelli & Durrett, 1998)*

| Emerging Skill | Space | Equipment |
|---|---|---|
| **Crawling** | • Variety of surfaces to crawl on (carpet, smooth tile, texture blankets, bubble wrap taped to floor, grass)<br>• Something to crawl to: YOU, window or mirror close to floor, fish tank (behind Plexiglass cupboard door) | • Balls to crawl after<br>• Tunnels or other interesting places to crawl through (e.g., table draped with blanket)<br>• Partially curtained alcoves to crawl into |
| **Pulling up Standing Cruising** | • Sturdy furniture that will not tip over (e.g., sofa)<br>• Railing securely fastened to wall at child's height<br>• Something to pull up to: mirror or window | • Standers with casters |
| **Walking** | • Clear pathways<br>• Smooth surfaces (no loose rugs to trip over)<br>• Challenging obstacles for more experienced walkers (e.g., a wooden ladder laid out on the floor where children can step over rungs) | • Sturdy push toys (shopping carts or baby buggies with 4 wheels)<br>• Pull toys<br>• Wagons<br>• Simple riding toys propelled by pushing feet along ground<br>• More advanced riding toys propelled by pedaling |
| **Running** | • Sufficient open space without tripping hazards<br>• Adults and other children to run after<br>• Ideally, a protected outdoor space available as needed rather than according to a rigid schedule | • Balls<br>• Simple kites<br>• Scarves |
| **Climbing** | • Varied elevations within structure of room: lofts, platforms, play pits<br>• Built-in climbing structures with padded surfaces beneath<br>• Mirror behind climber so children can watch themselves climb | • Vinyl-covered foam shapes that can be configured as climbing areas<br>• Ramps, slides, and stairs with room for two or more children to ascend and descend together |

## Play With People

Play with other people develops alongside of, and eventually intertwines with, babies' play with objects and movement. Like those types of play, it has its roots in the earliest weeks of life. Within the first few months, babies perk up and seem to focus when familiar voices address them. Soon, they begin to smile and respond to adults' vocalizations with their own sounds. This milestone is celebrated and nurtured in many cultures with a variety of games and rituals that involve touching babies—sometimes along with naming body parts—and culminate in tickling. At first, the babies derive enjoyment from the sensations of touch, sound, and tickling. The pleasure intensifies as babies learn to recognize the pattern of sound and touch and to anticipate the tickling that it portends.

Developing your own repertoire of these types of games will help you fulfill your role as one of the baby's first play partners. If you can ask older members of your family or community to share examples of the sorts of baby games they remember, you will make your collection of games more unique and personal at the same time that you learn something about your own cultural heritage.

A word of caution is in order here. Babies experience sensory input in very individual ways. A pleasant tickle for one might be overwhelming for another. You need to be very sensitive and alert to babies' cues—either that they enjoy the game and want more, or that they have had enough. Prolonged tickling, or tickling against a child's will, sends a message that the child is powerless. In this, as in all your interactions with babies, the key is to go slowly, asking in words and gestures what the baby would like, and pausing long enough for the baby to respond in some way.

As babies begin to formulate the idea that things continue to exist when out of sight, they take delight in games of "peek-a-boo." Variations include hiding a toy, hiding your face, or hiding the child's own face under a cloth. Covering a toy is less likely to cause distress than covering the child's face, which many babies find intolerable. You can initiate the game as a child plays with a toy by covering the toy and asking, "Where's the teddy bear?" and then quickly pulling the cloth away with the exclamation, "There it is!" If this elicits smiles or giggles, you can progress, perhaps another day, to covering your own face and "reappearing." Gradually, you can let the child control more of the game, first by being the one to pull the cloth away, and then by performing both steps of covering and uncovering.

Many babies enjoy "give and take" games. "Give mommy the keys," said in an expectant tone, with accompanying outstretched hand, usually results in a quizzical look and tentative proffering of the requested item. The fun begins when this action is met with exaggerated exclamations of thanks and, more important, when the roles are reversed so that the baby becomes the recipient of the keys.

As babies gain mobility, their play begins to incorporate their new skills. Proficient crawlers will enjoy crawling after (or away from!) you in simple chase games. When they first become upright, they will probably need to devote all their energy and attention to maintaining that position, but as they grow more comfortable in it they will again delight in chasing and being chased. "I'm going to get you!" seems to be an almost universal signal guaranteed to elicit squeals of laughter.

While adults are babies' first play partners, the role of peers increases throughout the first three years of life. Young infants may respond to each other simply by looking, then by smiling or vocalizing. Lacking expertise, babies' earliest attempts to play with peers may consist of exploratory touches (which the recipient may not welcome), or offering and taking toys or other objects. Adults who recognize these gestures as play will support them rather than imposing adult interpretations of personal space or ownership. You can compliment a child for "gentle touching" or strategically position your body to intercept more rambunctious efforts. If you notice Daniel looking shocked that Sam has grabbed a ball from his hands, you may be able to turn a potential conflict into a game by saying, "Uh oh! Sam has the ball. Give it back to Daniel, Sam." Sam, of course, will be more likely to go along with this scenario if he has previously enjoyed similar interactions with you. The reward comes when toddlers are able to move beyond these ritualized exchanges and take part in their own give-and-take or chasing games (O'Brien, 1997).

## Pretend Play

The earliest dramatic play may consist of pretending to drink from a cup or take a bite from a picture of an apple. Later, babies move toward pretending with other children, perhaps imitating another child patting a baby doll, for example, or joining a group of children who are all pretending individually to eat lunch. True cooperative play, where, for example, one child is "Doctor" and another is "Patient," is a fairly sophisticated accomplishment. While children are developing this skill, it is up to adults to support toddlers' pretend play by filling the role of a cooperative play partner. You can be the long-suffering "Patient" who is attended by several enthusiastic doctors. Or you can help children coordinate their play by narrating what you observe: "Two mommies are rocking their babies to sleep. Shh."

Another way to support pretend play is by providing props. It is generally believed that the younger the child, the more realistic the props need to be. This holds true for older children as well, if they happen to have had very little play experience. For accomplished preschool players, a stick can be a horse, a crutch, a sword, or a magic wand. Toddlers, who might readily carry on long conversations with "Grandma" on a realistic toy telephone, are probably unable to use a block as a substitute.

Bronson (1995) recommends that the materials available to support pretend play become gradually more complex, beginning with dolls and stuffed animals for infants, and adding telephones, unbreakable dishes, and cleaning tools as children grow. A beginner at role-play, satisfied with carrying a big purse and clattering around in adult shoes, will appreciate more elaborate accessories, like dresses, gloves, and vests as he or she has more practice. As children grow more expert at wrapping dolls in blankets and giving them bottles, you can add simple doll clothing with easy fasteners. Expand the housekeeping tools available and encourage more complex play themes by filling in the details: pots and pans, spoons and spatulas, dustcloths, dustpans, mops, iron and ironing board.

The props need to reflect the children's actual lives if they are to use them to act out their understanding. If they have never seen anyone ironing, they will have little idea of what to do with your toy iron and ironing board. That means you need to be familiar with their home environments to some extent. One way you can accomplish this is by asking parents for suggestions and donations.

## Play With Language

Play with language is closely related to pretend play, since both involve the use of symbols or substitutes for actual objects. Naming games are one example of such play and, like other types of play, they evolve as children mature, becoming more complex and more child-driven. Recall the game in which an adult touches and names the parts of the baby's face. As soon as babies seem to understand the language, the game becomes one of asking them, "Where's your eye? Where's your nose?" And this progresses to asking them to produce the name when you point to their nose: "What's this?" Objects in the room or other people also provide categories of things to be named, or to be pointed to when you name them. You can ask a child, "Who's that?" as you point to each child in turn. Playful children sometimes get into the spirit and turn the tables on their questioners, pointing to you and asking, "Who's that?"

Children with disabilities may require special supports to use language in their play, such as picture boards or switches to activate simple voice recordings ("catch me!"). They can benefit from adults modeling useful words and phrases: "It's my turn" or "All fall down!"

Play with language includes an enjoyment of books and stories. The types of books recommended for children with disabilities share the same characteristics enjoyed by other infants and toddlers. Images of familiar objects, including photographs of people and things in the child's environment, provide opportunities for the kind of give-and-take described above. Repetition of key phrases at intervals within the story inspires a delightful sense of anticipation and encourages children to say them with the adult. Book versions of familiar songs are another way of encouraging children to participate in "reading" the story. Books can be made more manageable for children with physical challenges by attaching them to a stable surface with Velcro and adding tabs or "fluffers" to make it easier to turn pages.

## Conclusion

One barrier to inclusion of children with disabilities in child care programs can be fear on the part of providers that they won't know what to do, that they won't be able to handle the extra responsibility, even that they might somehow inadvertently cause harm by doing the wrong thing. This chapter has tried to make the case that children with disabilities are children first, sharing the needs of all children for safety, security, and exploration. Providers with a solid understanding of child development are making a valuable contribution to the welfare of children with disabilities when they simply practice elements of good, responsive caregiving. Of course, accommodations and adaptations will be needed, but when viewed in the context of the flexibility required of all infant-toddler caregivers, those will seem less overwhelming. It will also help to remember that being an inclusive child care provider does not mean knowing everything there is to know about every—or even any—disability. While there are many resources caregivers can tap to learn about specific disabilities (see, for example, Paasche, Gorrill, & Strom, 2004), here again, principles of best practice for *all* children apply. As every skilled provider knows, the caregiver cannot succeed in isolation. Close partnerships with parents are essential for caregivers of *all* children; for those serving children with disabilities, the network of partnerships is expanded to include therapists and other professionals with specialized knowledge. The idea is not to turn child care providers into therapists, but rather to extend the benefit of their skills to *all* children.

## References

Ainsworth, M. D. (1967). *Infancy in Uganda: Infant care and the growth of love.* Baltimore: The Johns Hopkins Press.

Bowlby, J. (1989). *Secure and insecure attachment.* New York: Basic Books.

Bronson, M. B. (1995). *The right stuff for children birth to 8: Selecting play materials to support development.* Washington, DC: National Association for the Education of Young Children.

Cryer, D. (2000). The whole child: Transdisciplinary implications for infant and toddler care. In D. Cryer & T. Harms (Eds.), *Infants and toddlers in out-of-home care* (pp. 351-364). Baltimore: Paul H. Brookes.

Gerber, M. (1998). *Dear parent: Caring for infants with respect.* Los Angeles: Resources for Infant Educarers.

Gunnar, M. R. (1996). *Quality of care and the buffering of stress physiology: Its potential in protecting the developing human brain.* Minneapolis, MN: University of Minnesota Institute of Child Development.

Guralnick, M. J. (2000). The early intervention system and out-of-home child care. In D. Cryer and T. Harms (Eds.), *Infants and toddlers in out-of-home care* (pp.207-234). Baltimore: Paul H. Brookes.

Keogh, J., & Sugden, D. (1985). *Movement skill development.* New York: Macmillan.

Lally, J. R., Griffin, A., Fenichel, E., Segal, M. M., Szanton, E. S., & Weissbourd, B. (1995). *Caring for infants and toddlers in groups: Developmentally appropriate practice.* Arlington, VA: Zero to Three.

Linder, T, W. (1993). *Transdisciplinary play-based assessment: A functional approach to working with young children.* Baltimore: Paul H. Brookes.

O'Brien, M. (1998). *Inclusive child care for infants and toddlers: Meeting individual and special needs.* Baltimore: Paul H. Brookes.

Paasche, C. L., Gorrill, L., & Strom, B. (2004). *Children with special needs in early childhood settings: Identification, intervention, inclusion.* Clifton Park, NY: Delmar Learning.

Raikes, H. (1996). A secure base for babies: Applying attachment concepts to the infant care setting. *Young Children, 51*(5), 59-67.

Stroufe, L. A. 91995). *Emotional development: The organization of emotional life in the early years.* Cambridge, UK: Cambridge University Press.

Torelli, L., & Durrett, C. (1998). *Landscapes for learning: Designing group care environments for infants, toddlers, and two-year-olds.* Berkeley, CA: Spaces for Children.

## Case Study

*You would like to get Julius interacting at the centers with his peers. You and his parents have been doing a lot of work with Julius to help him decrease his tactile sensitivity. He enjoys soft cushiony material but has always been adverse to getting his hands dirty or playing with coarser materials. Lately, he has been playing with sand on a tray attached to his chair. Julius is now able to pour it back and forth between stacking cups, and he enjoys dragging his finger through the sand.*

### Questions

1. What type of activities could you envision Julius doing with a peer that would involve sand? Where would it take place? How would you introduce it?

2. How would you progress to an activity that involved two or three peers? What changes would need to be made?

3. What other activities could help Julius with his tactile sensitivity?

# Chapter 3

# The Preschool Years, Ages 3-4

*Mark Brown*

*Three preschoolers enter the woodworking learning center. Charles, a 4-year-old with delays in fine motor/adaptive skills and with social-emotional concerns, approaches the table first. Sara and Breena, both also 4 years old, follow Charles. Mrs. Green is seated in a chair next to the table. She looks directly at Breena and says, "Do you want to work here?" Breena nods affirmatively. Mrs. Green positions both a hammer and a block of wood on the table and then looks at Breena and says, "OK, there you go. . . . I'll move this [plastic hammer] out of the way." She then tells Charles, "You can hammer with this [plastic hammer and wooden golf tees] on the block of Styrofoam while you wait for one of them to be finished."*

*Mrs. Green picks up another large block of wood and places it on the table directly in front of Sara. Sara, who is standing five feet away from Charles, begins hitting her metal nail into the piece of wood. Breena, who is standing on the opposite side of Sara, looks at Charles, but doesn't use her hammer. Charles takes a pair of goggles off the table and places them over his eyes. He then picks up the metal hammer not being used by Breena and hits a metal nail that is already embedded in a block of wood. Mrs. Green looks at Charles and says, "What are you going to make?" Charles doesn't respond. He keeps hitting the nail with his hammer.*

When given the option of using a plastic or wooden hammer, Charles chose to "try" a regular hammer. Mrs. Green initially made a material adaptation (i.e., offering a plastic hammer and wooden golf tees) for Charles, so he would not become frustrated with this task. He was still developing readiness skills in the areas of eye-hand coordination and fine motor skills, and Mrs. Green wanted him to try the activity with materials that would not require as much skill. As children are allowed to make sense out of their immediate surroundings, they are able to successfully build upon their own self-concept. Appropriate environments are more likely to facilitate verbal skills that may lead to improved language development through child dialogue and child-peer engagement (Dunn, Beach, & Kontos, 1994). Preschool classrooms that allow children to choose which learning center materials to use and manipulate may facilitate greater creative thinking as well as more complex behaviors in the context of material/activity exploration (Reinhartsen, Garfinkle, & Wolery, 2002). This exploration could occur individually or with peers. Some teachers, faced with the push-down approach to curriculum, find it difficult to maintain the flexibility and freedom found in effective early childhood programs.

While teachers can create effective adaptations with materials that children use at specific learning centers, they also should allow preschoolers the opportunity to choose whether or not to use those materials. Allowing a child to make that decision may increase his level of engagement with that particular play object as well as allow him to learn more complex play patterns over time (Reinhartsen, Garfinkle, & Wolery, 2002). In addition, because the preschooler with a delay or disability is demonstrating competent play behaviors, his peers may be more likely to parallel play with him or involve him in their group play activities. The ability to effectively "play," with adult and/or peer prompting when needed, with other peers is a practice that can lead to greater social, emotional, and cognitive development over time for the preschool child (Bredekamp & Copple, 1997).

The early childhood educator and early childhood intervention specialist must envision each child as unique with differing experiences and interests. Yet, as a class, these preschoolers belong to a community of young learners who are eager to explore their learning center environments independently, with another peer, or in a group of children. In addition, preschoolers are more willing to work with other peers who may be perceived as being different if the preschool teachers are accepting of those differences and promote the uniqueness of all who come to learn in that community (Roberts & Lindsell, 1997; Roberts & Smith, 1999).

In the context of peer interaction in a preschool setting, play can be viewed as a multifaceted event or activity. An adult might ask a preschooler what he or she is doing when observing the child stacking cardboard blocks on top of each other. The preschooler might say, "I'm building a fortress." Children who are in a group may state the universal comment, "We're playing," which is just another way of saying, "We are learning and having fun at the same time." In the context of a child-initiated play event, preschoolers often make choices with regard to the learning center activity they wish to participate in. Children may gravitate towards a particular learning center activity (e.g., making a collage) that allows for greater peer involvement, problem solving, or self-exploration. Play should be viewed as a social event that supports the following ideals (Smith & Croom, 2000):

• **Play Is Meaningful:** Play behavior is developmental in nature and directly related to a child's ability to demonstrate both cognitive and communicative skills (Shore, O'Connell, & Bates, 1984). Children with or without delays often can construct meaning in their play, either independently or with peers. Children also may develop themes or a script (e.g., making dinner or feeding the baby) in the context of a play event.

• **Play Is Symbolic:** A preschooler's play can be viewed as a compilation of one's prior experiences. It should be no surprise that children develop patterns of play to validate activities that may have occurred in the past, but are still meaningful to them in the present.

• **Play Is Rule-governed:** During the preschool years, children begin to make rules for their play. These rules may be unspoken and demonstrated through facial expressions, hand gestures, and activity pace. Conversely, these rules also may be spoken and demonstrated by statements. At a "magic castle" learning center, for example, a child could say, "You have to have your hat on when you enter the castle" or "First, you have to climb up the ladder and then go inside."

• **Play Is Pleasurable:** Preschoolers will often let an adult know the level of satisfaction they receive from their social interaction in a particular learning center. This level of satisfaction can be demonstrated through a sustained period of play engagement. Children also may be further connected to an activity based upon commonality statements or similar behaviors and/or movements that demonstrate that they are working towards the same goal. If an activity is not pleasurable for a child, then it should not be considered play. When play is child-constructed, it becomes more intrinsically motivating for the child to repeat or build upon prior play behaviors that are meaningful (whether those attempts at play are done independently or with other peers).

## Environmental Influences on Play

The environment in which preschool children play and interact must be examined. Typically developing children and children with delays/disabilities must have equal access to learning centers and the various activities that take place within each center. How a learning center environment is set up determines the level and variability of play behaviors that typical children and children with delays can demonstrate. Rettig (1998) addressed five environmental variables that influence the play behavior of young children. They are categorized as follows:

• **Theoretical Orientation of the Program.** This often pertains to the degree of structure in the early childhood preschool program. Preschool early childhood educators and early childhood intervention specialists are more likely to observe children with delays demonstrating more "pretend" play during free play as opposed to during structured play activities.

• **Design of the Preschool Classroom.** Preschool classrooms should allow for child movement within a learning center as well as movement between centers. A child with limited mobility and a fine/gross motor delay should be able to move comfortably between centers as well as move and use materials effectively within a learning center environment. Creating a learning center environment that is open and has accessible materials may encourage students to maintain an age-appropriate play behavior over an extended period of time.

• **Learning Center Arrangement.** Learning center activities should be "leveled" through the use of pre-academic and environmental accommodations/modifications and adaptations to address the developmental needs of a variety of preschoolers. In addition, preschoolers need to feel that they can play with their peers with limited distractions. When incompatible learning centers are placed together, interaction problems among children are likely to manifest. A child who is nonverbal and wishes to communicate (e.g., using sign language or a picture communication system) with another typically developing peer is less likely to have a communication breakdown if the learning center area is not located near other areas (e.g., dress-up or housekeeping) that promote high activity or frequent peer movement.

• **Length of Play Period.** Early childhood educators and early childhood intervention specialists agree that typically developing preschoolers and preschoolers with delays/disabilities need to be in an environment where the potential for social interaction and peer-related play is relatively high. A children's level of maturity and developmental skill level will determine the types of play behaviors (e.g., associative versus cooperative) that are demonstrated. Preschool teachers should be encouraged to develop longer scheduling consistency so that children are made cognizant of specific times for both small-group and large-group activities. Preschool teachers should allow for longer play periods for students with delays who are being taught in an inclusive setting. Longer play periods increase the opportunity for longer play engagement and more complex play behaviors to be demonstrated over time.

• **Effects of Social Versus Isolate Toys.** Research has demonstrated that social toys (i.e., blocks, balls, and puppets) should be used with preschoolers with general delays in an inclusive setting. These toys may be more likely to encourage and maintain play behavior between two or more children (Ivory & McCollum, 1999; Reinhartsen, Garfinkle, & Wolery, 2002). Children with more serious delays in the area of communication, cognition, and fine motor skills should be given the opportunity for choice-making with regard to toys and materials. Allowing children the opportunity to pick toys and/or materials in a learning center may facilitate socially appropriate behaviors. As children are allowed to explore their own interests, sustained play/social behaviors with a favorite object and increased complexity with regard to toy or classroom material usage may increase over time (Cole & Levinson, 2002).

## Material Adaptations, Environmental and Instructional Accommodations, and Peer-to-Peer Support

The role of the early childhood educator and the early childhood special education intervention specialist should be one of collaborator. Any material adaptations; curriculum modifications; or environmental, instructional, and assessment accommodations that are created could benefit other preschool children in the inclusive classroom.

Traditionally, preschool classrooms are set up by using the center approach. Using this premise, this chapter will present material adaptations, environmental and instructional accommodations, and peer-to-peer support strategies that specifically address preschoolers with mild to severe delays in the following developmental areas: 1) cognition, 2) communication, 3) fine/gross motor, 4) self-help/adaptive, and 5) social/emotional development (Gould & Sullivan, 1999; McDonnell, Nelson, & Malmskog, 2003).

In the book center, the following adaptations and accommodations could be provided for preschool children in an inclusive classroom. With regard to material adaptations, the teacher could provide a board made of either flannel or cloth with Velcro attachments, so that preschoolers can re-create their stories with cloth story props that can be placed on the board. This strategy would benefit a child with delays in communication or fine-motor skills, as well as a child with social-emotional concerns, who could possibly problem-solve a story event using the story props or act out a social story. With regard to environmental accommodations, the teacher could provide opportunities for the preschooler to be exposed to "environmental" print (e.g., golden arches representing a McDonald's restaurant) seen in the neighborhood. With regard to instructional accommodations, the teacher could provide earphones and a tape recorder for preschoolers who wish to share a reading book at a table.

In the block center area, the preschool teacher could incorporate a picture communication system to allow a nonverbal child to participate in making requests and taking turns with other peers. With regard to environmental accommodations, the preschool teacher could allow the child to build an object, using the wall for necessary support. The object could be built either horizontally or vertically. With regard to environmental accommodations, the preschool teacher could incorporate the use of perforated colored tape to set up building block boundaries for a child who has social-emotional concerns or is auditorally defensive.

In the water table learning center, the preschool teacher could provide a choice of materials. With regard to peer-to-peer support, the preschool teacher could incorporate objects that require peers to work together towards a common goal (e.g., filling plastic cups with water and then pouring the water into a one-gallon container until it is half full). For a material adaptation, the preschool teacher could provide toys that are easy to grasp, have handles, or are textured for better manipulation.

In the dramatic play center, the preschool teacher could incorporate clothing that is easy to get into and easy to get out of, such as attire with Velcro snaps that children could put on by themselves. To address environmental accommodations, the preschool teacher could allow for wide spaces in the dress-up area that accommodate children with social-emotional concerns as well as problems in ambulation. For an instructional accommodation, the teacher could place enlarged digital pictures of peers in various clothing on the wall to serve as examples of possible outfits to wear in the center.

In the cooking center, the preschool teacher could create directional posters that allow two or more children to follow a sequence of cooking directions. Sequenced recipe cards will allow a child with a delay in communication to communicate more easily to an adult or peer the steps needed to create the final food product. Peers could assist in manipulating a rolling pin, flattening the cookie dough, and/or organizing plastic utensils in their tray area.

Post digital pictures on the wall of the computer center to demonstrate directions for using the computer correctly. With regard to environmental accommodations, the preschool teacher could allow for the repositioning of the computer table to accommodate a child with gross motor delays (e.g., one who uses a wheelchair or a walker). Making a sign-up sheet on which children can write the letters of their name or use a stamp to record their presence in a particular center would enable young children to practice recognizing and/or printing their names.

In the writing learning center, provide a variety (different sizes, shapes, and textures) of writing instruments. Gaining experience in writing on different surfaces and in different postures (e.g., sitting and standing) is also very important.

In the art learning center, label containers graphically and in print for easy identification. They also should be positioned for easy access. Children should experience painting and drawing on different surfaces and using different textures. Creating physical "boundaries" for an art project (i.e., children can develop an art project in a box lid or a plastic tray) would help many children maintain control of their paper and prevent extremely messy situations. You will need a variety of art materials that provide the opportunity to manipulate various shapes, sizes, textures, and colors.

Material adaptations, environmental and instructional accommodations, and peer-to-peer support are child-centered strategies that allow a preschooler with a delay or disability to interact with his classmates in the context of a play-related event. Through careful observation of a preschooler's behavior at the various learning centers, the early childhood educator and early childhood intervention specialist can develop opportunities for play that stimulate the emotional, social, and cognitive development of a preschooler in an inclusive setting.

The preschool teacher can informally assess learning center play behaviors that are demonstrated by a child with a developmental delay or disability. This is done so that the child can demonstrate emotional growth and cognitive/physical development through play-related activities at the various learning centers. This chapter's next section will discuss arena-style assessment and practices.

## Assessment Practices and the Preschool Child

The purpose of informal assessment is to provide the early childhood educator, and possibly a team of professionals, a common understanding of a child's typical behaviors and present levels of functioning with regard to her developmental, sensorimotor, cognitive, communicative, social, and emotional functioning (Spenciner & Cohen, 2003). Two assessment practices commonly used with preschool children are arena-style, play-based assessment and portfolios.

## Arena-Style Assessment

For the purpose of this chapter, the transdisciplinary model for arena-style, play-based assessment will be discussed (Hooper & Umansky, 2004). In the transdisciplinary model, a key facilitator plays with the child while the other team members watch and take notes. Each team member is aware of her peers' roles in this process. The team members come together to share information with other members and the child's parent in order to determine a specific plan of intervention.

In transdisciplinary arena-style assessment, the team of evaluators may include the child's parents, an early childhood special education interventionist, an early childhood educator, a speech therapist, an occupational therapist, and a physical therapist. Through the process of observation, the examiners are able to see the child develop a level of comfort, because play is occurring in a familiar setting (Linder, 1993). Also, the assessment team can see how the child plays with toys independently or interacts with another peer during a cooperative activity.

Related service professionals who are trained to work with children with disabilities and delays include the speech and language pathologist (SLP), the occupational therapist (OT), and the physical therapist (PT). The speech and language pathologist's role is to assist young children with mild to severe delays in communication; teaching them, for example, how to speak in an age-appropriate manner, with or without assistive technology. The occupational therapist's role is to help young children with social-emotional or fine motor concerns perform more functional tasks, such as self-grooming, or life skills, such as dressing, holding a crayon, or setting the table. They also work with students who have sensory integration issues. The physical therapist's role is to help a child sustain muscle development in order to build upon muscle growth, as well as facilitate motor skill acquisition, motor skill movement, and proper body posture (Bowe, 2000; Hooper & Umansky, 2004).

The speech and language pathologist usually serves as the main examiner in arena-style assessment process. The examiner can assess the child in either a low-structured or highly structured environment. The former assessment environment allows the child to play with toys and materials of his own choosing. The latter assessment environment allows the examiner to dictate the child's play patterns. The examiner may have to redirect the child's play behavior through a prompting procedure.

Parents play an important role in transdisciplinary arena-style assessment. A parent also can participate in a play activity and serve as both play facilitator and play interpreter. The team also might ask the parent to engage with the child in play behaviors that normally occur at home. Early childhood preschool teachers and service providers then can ascertain developmental areas that need to be further examined for future program planning (Myers, McBride, & Peterson, 1996).

## Incorporating Portfolio Assessment in an Early Childhood Setting

A portfolio is a collection of a child's work that has been gathered over a period that can illustrate the pre-academic and social development of a preschooler. Materials placed into a portfolio can demonstrate the particular strengths that children with delays or disabilities demonstrate in the classroom, at home, or in their community (Dunst, 2000).

Portfolios have many advantages. The creation of a portfolio that clearly demonstrates developmental growth can facilitate bolstering a child's self-esteem, particularly for young children with developmental delays (Arter & Spandel, 1991; Campbell, Milbourne, & Silverman, 2001). A preschool teacher can use a child's portfolio to triangulate informal or formal assessment data, because it serves as an authentic representation of the child's developmental skill level at a particular time. Finally, information gathered from a portfolio may appear less threatening than a formal assessment test because it serves as a more "naturalistic" permanent product (Meyer, Shuman, & Angello, 1990). The child-made materials that are placed into a preschooler's portfolio can be organized according to the following developmental domains (Meisels & Steele, 1991):

- **Fine/Gross Motor Movement:** Samples of a child's handwriting over time on a "sign-up sheet" that is used at a particular learning center (e.g., the computer station). Digital video of a child with a gross motor delay demonstrating correct posture with the use of a walker at a learning center.
- **Communication:** A series of videotapes taken over time that demonstrate the child's language skill development when he communicates through puppets at the puppet theater. Samples of mastered sight word vocabulary that were once part of the preschool child's word wall. Copies of pictures used in the picture communication system.
- **Social-emotional:** Disposition cards that the child displays to demonstrate an awareness of his feelings in a specific context. Digital video to capture a child demonstrating effective "toy sharing" skills at a learning center.

The following issues must be addressed with regard to the effective use of portfolio assessment in the early childhood inclusive classroom. Issue one pertains to making sure that materials placed in the child's portfolio are valid. The chosen materials must demonstrate what the child can accomplish in a naturalistic manner at a specific learning center. If prompts (i.e., verbal gestures) are used to elicit a specific child action or behavior, they must be noted in the teacher's comments. Issue two pertains to the criteria used to examine and select materials that will be placed into a child's portfolio. The criteria used must be consistent. In addition, its continued usage also must be agreed upon by both the teacher and the child's parent. Issue three pertains to the manner in which the developmental growth of a child's portfolio is measured.

Spenciner and Cohen (2003) suggest the use of preschool teacher narratives that delineate the child's strengths and limitations in the creation and development of materials. Scaled scoring (e.g., from 1 to 4) can be incorporated when a child has multiple materials to assess in one development domain. Descriptors also can be added to the score to allow for greater clarity. Finally, a rubric could be incorporated to lend more specificity to the scores representing materials components.

In conclusion, preschool teachers should strive to become more aware of authentic assessment procedures that allow them to measure children's developmental capabilities in a naturalistic and less intrusive format. Children's play, which serves as a framework for authentic assessment, should be facilitated through material adaptations; environmental, instructional, and assessment accommodations; and peer-to-peer support strategies. Information that is gathered through teacher observation and then recorded should be directly related back to teacher instruction, in order to promote and sustain continued development for a child with delays or disabilities in an inclusive preschool setting.

# References

Arter, J. A., & Spandel, V. (1991). *Using portfolios of student work in instruction and assessment*. Portland, OR: Northwest Regional Educational Laboratory.

Bowe, F. G. (2000). *Birth to five: Early childhood special education* (3rd ed.). Albany, NY: Delmar.

Bredekamp, S., & Copple, C. (Eds.). (1997). *Developmentally appropriate practices in early childhood programs* (rev. ed.). Washington, DC: National Association for the Education of Young Children.

Campbell, P. H., Milbourne, S. A., & Silverman, C. (2001). Strengths-based child portfolios: A professional development activity to alter perspectives of children with special needs. *Topics in Early Childhood Special Education, 21*(3), 152-161.

Cole, C. L., & Levison, T. T. (2002). Effects on within-activity choices on the challenging behavior of children with severe developmental disabilities. *Journal of Positive Behavior Intervention, 4,* 29-37.

Dunn, L., Beach, S. A., & Kontos, S. (1994). Quality of the literacy environment in day care and children's development. *Journal of Research in Childhood Education, 9,* 24-34.

Dunst, C. J. (2000). Revisiting "rethinking early intervention." *Topics in Early Childhood Special Education, 20,* 95-104.

Gould, P., & Sullivan, L. (1999). *The inclusive early childhood classroom: Easy ways to adapt learning centers for all children*. Beltsville, MD: Gryphon House.

Hooper, S. R., & Umansky, W. (2004). *Young children with special needs* (4th ed.). Columbus, OH: Merrill Prentice Hall.

Ivory, J. J., & McCollum, J. A. (1999). Effects of social and isolate toys on social play in inclusive settings. *Journal of Special Education, 32*(4), 238-243.

Linder, T. W. (1993). *Transdisciplinary play-based assessment: A functional approach to working with young children*. Baltimore: Paul H. Brookes.

McDonnell, A., Nelson, C., & Malmskog, S. (2003, December). *Strategies for increasing participation and peer interaction in inclusive preschool learning centers*. Paper presented at the 19th Annual DEC Conference on Young Children with Special Needs and their Families, Chicago, IL.

Meisels, S. A., & Steele, D. (1991). *The early childhood portfolio collection*. Ann Arbor, MI: University of Michigan Center for Human Growth and Potential.

Meyer, C., Schuman, S., & Angello, N. (1990). *Aggregating portfolio data* [white paper]. Lake Oswego, OR: Northwest Evaluation Association.

Myers, C. L., McBride, S. L., & Peterson, C. A. (1996). Transdisciplinary play-based assessment in early childhood special education: An examination of social validity. *Topics in Early Childhood Special Education, 16,* 102-116.

Reinhartsen, D. B., Garfinkle, A. N., & Wolery, M. (2002). Engagement with toys in two-year-old children with autism. Teacher selection versus child choice. *Research & Practice for Persons with Severe Disabilities, 27*(3), 175-187.

Rettig, M. (1998). Environmental influences on the play of young children with disabilities. *Education and Training in Mental Retardation, 33*(2), 189-194.

Roberts, C. M., & Lindsell, J. S. (1997). Children's attitudes and behavioural intentions toward peers with disabilities. *International Journal of Disability, Development, and Education, 44,* 113-145.

Roberts, C. M., & Smith, P. R. (1999). Attitudes and behavior of children towards peers with disabilities. *International Journal of Disability, Development and Education, 46*(1), 35-50.

Shore, C., O'Connell, B., & Bates, E. (1984). First sentences in language and symbolic play. *Developmental Psychology, 20*(5), 872-880.

Smith, K. E., & Croom, L. (2001). Mulitple dimensional self-concepts of children and teacher beliefs about developmentally appropriate practices. *Journal of Educational Research, 93*(5), 312-321.

Spenciner, L. J., & Cohen, L. G. (2003). *Assessment of children and youth with special needs*. Boston: Allyn and Bacon.

## Case Study

*Jason, a 4-year-old male with moderate delays in communication and cognition, and with ambulatory difficulties, is standing at the water table with Seth, a 4-year-old peer who is developing typically. Both preschoolers are wearing raincoats to keep from getting wet. There is a toy resting at the side of the table that has a plastic funnel at the top. The funnel is positioned directly over a red water wheel. There is also an empty 1-gallon jug at the water table.*

*Seth looks down and sees an empty 1-liter plastic water bottle floating in the water. He picks it up and fills it with water. Seth takes the 1-liter water bottle and pours its contents into the 1-gallon jug. Jason points at the 1-gallon jug that Seth is filling, and then picks up a small plastic container and begins to fill it with water. Jason lifts the toy with his right hand and pours the water from his plastic container into the funnel of the toy. The water enters the funnel and then falls directly on the water wheel, which begins to spin. Seth continues filling the 1-gallon jug, using his 1-liter water bottle. When the jug is completely full, he picks it up with both hands. Seth pours all of the water from the jug into the funnel. Jason looks at Seth, who doesn't respond, and then begins frantically pouring water from his plastic container into the funnel.*

*Jason attempts to assist Seth by holding the side of the jug. Both of them watch the water travel through the funnel and land on the wheel barrel, which starts to spin. When Seth empties his 1-gallon jug, he places it back in the water table. Seth then takes off his raincoat and walks to another center. Jason looks sad as his peer leaves the water table area. Jason looks around and follows Seth to the post office center, where they begin to decorate envelopes.*

## Questions

1. What nonverbal and verbal attempts did Jason make to create a reciprocal interaction with Seth? What developmental strengths did Jason demonstrate in his attempt to play with Seth?

2. What did this case study tell you about inclusion for children with delays who may have limited ways to communicate effectively with another typically developing peer in a learning center activity?

3. Suggest two environmental and instructional accommodations that you would implement to facilitate greater social interaction between Seth and Jason.

# Chapter 4

# The Kindergarten/ Primary Years, Ages 5-8

*Isabel Killoran and Sonia Mastrangelo*

*Lucia Dias is looking forward to her first year of teaching 2nd grade. She has spent the past four years teaching kindergarten and is ready for a change. Some of the children she had in kindergarten will be in her class this year, and she is eager to see how much they've grown. The principal gave her the class list early—she has four children receiving special education services and he wanted her to get a head start on setting up the classroom and planning the curriculum.*

*One of the children, Maxine, 7, has a significant nonverbal learning disability. Maxine was one of Lucia's kindergarten students, and Lucia remembers her as eager and pleasant but extremely challenged by transitions between centers and often in tussles with her classmates. Benjamin, 6, is a new student to the school. He has autism, is nonverbal, and uses a picture communication system (PCS). Lucia visited his class-room last year and completed a workshop on teaching children with autism spectrum disorders to read. Benjamin had many friends in his 1st-grade class and he is worried about leaving them. Danika, 7, is quite puzzling. Although she was born in Canada, Danika did not speak English when she started kindergarten. Usually, this is not a problem, but Danika did not pick up English as quickly as the other English language learners. In fact, by the end of kindergarten, Danika could only identify three letter sounds. Her hearing has been checked, and the ESL teacher has provided her with support for the past two years. Unfortunately, she is no longer eligible for this support. The school support team wanted to give Danika as much time as possible, but Lucia wonders if she should be tested for a learning disability. The last student is Raymond, age 7. Lucia is worried about him. He has attention deficit hyperactivity disorder (ADHD)[1] and is very impulsive. Raymond is bright and does well academically—that is, if he gets the work completed. Last April, his parents separated and there has been a steady decline in his behavior. He often lashes out at his peers and teachers. After being asked to return a book he had ripped out of a student's hands, Raymond picked up his desk and threw it across the room. In kindergarten, Raymond was very busy, but he was not destructive. He was eager to participate and he didn't mind being redirected. The way he is acting now is very different. Lucia is sure it has more to do with his family situation than with the ADHD.*

*As Lucia looks at her classroom, barren except for a table and 20 desks, she won-ders how she can make it inviting and welcoming to all of her students. Besides the four students with IEPs[2], another 16 will need her attention. Lucia decides that the first thing she is going to ask for is more tables. If they're not available, she'll have to push the desks together. Lucia loved the vibrancy and energy of her kindergarten room. The children were always engaged, although she did have to admit that sometimes it got a bit loud. She wants to keep her classroom active and has been doing some reading on the Project Approach and differentiating curriculum. Her goal is to apply both of these strategies, but she is feeling the pressure of the province-wide testing that takes place next year. Lucia begins with what she knows works. She goes to her car and unloads the large carpet scrap she got from the local flooring store. It will make a good area for their classroom meetings. Next, she will tackle the reading corner.*

Starting formal schooling can signal a dramatic shift in a child's understanding about what school is and how learning takes place. Prior to kindergarten, many children spend their days, or part of their days, in preschool and/or nursery programs that allow them to explore, experiment, and define what it is they would like to learn. However, their freedom is eroded as they enter the structure of formal schooling. Differences in academic, social, and behavioral expectations can make this transition difficult.

In this chapter, we have decided to group kindergarten with the primary years because we believe that much of what occurs in the primary grades is not appropriate and does not contribute to fostering critical thinking and creative learning (Bredekamp & Copple, 1997). This is particularly true when we consider the education that children with disabilities are receiving in these grades. Although this chapter will not extensively explore critical perspectives of developmentally appropriate practice, the authors nevertheless strongly recommend reading up on this topic (see, for example, works by the following authors: Cannella, Carta, Lubeck, Kessler, Swadener)

Many children with disabilities transition well into kindergarten but find themselves becoming increasingly segregated as they pass through the grades. It begins innocuously with short, specific interventions but progresses to full withdrawal for language and mathematics, if not more. For some children with severe disabilities, they are not even given the opportunity to begin the primary grades with their peers; they find themselves in segregated classrooms because of expectations that they cannot do the required work. We would argue that often the real reason for the placement is that the general education teacher does not feel prepared to work with children with disabilities, especially children with low incidence or severe disabilities. Adding to this, many believe that special educators are the only ones who can deliver programs to children with disabilities and, consequently, do not consider the option of supporting the child in the general education classroom. This chapter will attempt to address some of the significant characteristics of the kindergarten/primary classrooms, examine expectations, and discuss how children with disabilities can be educated with their peers in the general education classroom. Specifically, we will address the environmental set-up (including behavioral expectations), differentiating instruction, and opportunities for play.

## Environmental Set-up

The majority of kindergarten classrooms are set up with centers, areas at which students explore and learn about specific topics, practice pre-skills and skills, socialize with their peers, engage in imaginative and socio-dramatic play, or spend time alone listening to stories or reading books. Circle time, or a class meeting, begins each class. Space is made for flexible individual, small, and large groupings. Teachers believe in child-directed activities; they encourage experimentation with materials, letters, numbers, and sounds. The walls display the children's work and families are welcomed into the classroom. There is a lot of movement, talking, singing, and laughing.

Unfortunately, once children have completed kindergarten, these opportunities begin to dwindle. They are now in "big" school and they have to act and learn like "big people." Usually one of the first things to appear is the desk, and one of the first things to go is the center approach. Children's learning needs do not change so dramatically in the summer months between kindergarten and 1st grade that the rules and expectations of school need to completely change. Yet, suddenly children find themselves sitting at desks, possibly beside a peer if they're lucky. The comfort of the reading corner, where they used to curl up with a book, is gone. The listening center, loved by the many children who couldn't read and by those who needed some quiet time or time to refocus, is gone. The art materials are in cupboards and can be used only during art time or during a special activity. Places for movement, like the dress-up center, are gone, and the children are expected to spend much more time sitting and "working." The only real time to dance, jump, hop, skip, and move is at recess and during physical education.

We see 1st grade as the transition year. Most 1st-grade teachers hold on to constructivist beliefs about how children learn, although these are not always reflected in their practice. Science and social studies lessons will still focus on centers; some may even broach using projects. But the seriousness of studying mathematics and language arts is beginning to become much clearer to the students. They discover that there is a right way and a wrong way to write. The students have baskets of notebooks they write new words into every day and are tested on every week. It doesn't matter that they don't know what the word means, what it sounds like, or what it rhymes with—they still have to learn it. Some of the students can already read or have a great memory and they seem to do well. Others get most of the words right but they are not able to transfer these words into their writing or reading. And others, like Benjamin and Danika, never get them right. They practice at home, they try their best, but they just can't do it.

Lucia has begun to keep a spelling test chart, and everyone who gets a perfect score receives a sticker. Benjamin and Danika are the only two without stickers and they have already learned that no matter how much they practice at home, it won't make any difference. Although Lucia has read about differentiating curriculum, she hasn't really given it much thought yet. She wonders how hard the work can be. It's only the 2nd grade! If we know that there can be upwards of four grade levels of ability in one classroom, why wouldn't we expect to see quite a significant spread in the early primary grades? Children in these grades need to have differentiated instruction just as much as those in the higher grades do. In fact, by not providing this support, young children are in danger of developing learned helplessness and of losing their self-esteem.

Benjamin's mother comes in to talk with Lucia about the spelling chart. She describes how eager her son was when he began studying the words only a month ago. Now, he won't even pull out his notebook. When Benjamin's mom asks him to practice, he cries that he is "dumb." Lucia is shocked. She really thought that the stickers would motivate the students. Devon is always talking about the chart, but he has the most stickers. It suddenly dawns on Lucia that no matter what she provides as a motivator to a student, if he is not capable of doing the task, he will not be able to do it. Tomorrow during their class meeting, she will tell the students she has decided to end the chart, and she will tell them why.

The next day, Lucia is pleasantly surprised by the students' understanding of how those who have fewer stickers may feel. She tells them that she is no longer going to ask them to memorize words; however, she still wants them to be able to practice letters, sounds, and words. The word wall will be added to regularly so the children can look there if they need to know how to spell something. Lucia asks them to make suggestions about how to make spelling time more fun. Raymond becomes quite excited when he suggests having a sandbox in which to write letters and words. Lucia decides to make spelling time activity-based. Children will be able to pick the activities they most enjoy, along with the ones Lucia asks them all to complete. She will make sure to include activities that address the needs and tap into the strengths of auditory, visual, and tactile/kinesthetic learners. This approach will free her up to work individually and in small groups with the students who need attention. She will be able to do more intensive phonemic awareness activities with those who need it, as well as spend time with those who need enrichment. Three of her students already can read on their own the chapter books she reads to the class. They rarely have time to read independently, however, because Lucia does not have a class-wide silent reading time. This new approach will give them some time to read and talk about the books and then work on related activities.

Lucia has quickly learned that the children must be given opportunity for movement many times throughout the day. They really can only sit focused for 15 minutes at a time without getting too fidgety. For example, Lucia incorporates movement into the transitions between activities. When she is ready for the children to move, either to a new activity or to their seats, she plays some gentle music. They are welcome to move any way they wish during the transition as long as they stop when the music stops and they keep their hands and feet to themselves. Every day, right before math activities, she implements a more vigorous activity for two minutes. Sometimes, they play Simon Says, sometimes a child leads the class in stretches and movements, and sometimes they just dance. Almost all of the students have taken the opportunity to lead the class. Benjamin's mom helped him program his switch to give directions to the students when it was his turn.

The temptation to have children in the primary grades stay at their desks or their tables for extended periods gets stronger as they progress through the grades. By the 3rd grade, much of what made the kindergarten classroom such an exciting place to be is gone. Teachers' expectations have changed and so have their approaches. Some of this is understandable, based solely on the developmental levels and abilities of the students; but some of it is due to a misunderstanding of what good teaching and active learning looks like at this stage.

### Changes in Expectations

Lucia thinks back to her kindergarten classroom and to her expectations of the children. She didn't feel any pressure to rush the children, and she viewed their "mistaken" behaviors (Gartrell, 2004) as teachable moments. Now there is a rigorous curriculum to complete, one that has expectations that have been pushed down from higher grades. There is pressure to have all of the students reading and writing well so that they will be prepared for 3rd grade and the standardized test. Lucia makes a list of how she envisions the 2nd grade as different from kindergarten.

- Children need to be able to read independently
- Lessons are longer, so the children need to remain seated for longer periods of time
- Students will have fewer choices

- Centers and the Project Approach (Katz & Chard, 2000) will be used only for science and social studies lessons
- Children need to be responsible for bringing their agendas back and forth, and for completing homework
- There will be a greater demand to write legibly and conventionally
- There will be less opportunity for movement, songs, and creative activities.

Lucia worries about how she is going to help Benjamin, Danika, Raymond, and Maxine meet these expectations. How will she find time to work with them and program for them individually? Lucia makes an appointment with Sophia, the special education resource teacher at her school, to talk about the accommodations, modifications, and adaptations she will need to make so everyone has a successful year. It is only October and so there is still plenty of time to make changes.

Sophia greets Lucia enthusiastically and is eager to collaborate on some overall strategies that will help her class transition smoothly. Sophia questions some of Lucia's expectations, such as fewer choices and less time to use centers. Maybe there is a way that Lucia can keep child-directed, active learning a key component of her program without sacrificing curriculum expectations. Sophia believes that differentiating instruction is the key.

> Differentiation—one facet of expert teaching—reminds us that [high-quality curriculum and instruction[3]] are unlikely to happen for the full range of students unless curriculum and instruction fit each individual, unless students have choices about what to learn and how, unless students take part in setting learning goals, and unless the classroom connects with the experiences and interest of the individual. (Tomlinson, 2000, p. 7)

**Accommodating Students' Needs Through Differentiating Instruction**
Lucia can differentiate instruction through content (what students learn), process (how students make sense of the information), and product (how students demonstrate what they have learned) (Tomlinson, 2001, p. 4). If she remembers to keep in mind the readiness level, interests, learning style, life circumstances, and experiences of each student while planning, Lucia will be able to create lessons, activities, and assessments that are good matches (Tomlinson, 2000). Sophia explains that although the students get what they each need, differentiation is not the same thing as individualization, as Lucia was imagining when she wrote up her expectations. Rather than spending a few minutes with each student, flexible grouping will allow Lucia to spend more time with them and get a better sense of their progress. This makes a lot of sense to Lucia. Raymond would be able to work at an enriched level with his peers, which might keep him more engaged and less likely to act out. The others are at the expected grade level, although Maxine and Benjamin struggle with concepts that are more abstract. Danika will need to have directions put on graphic organizers. Actually, using visuals will benefit many of the students in the class, and Lucia files this strategy away as something she needs to use more regularly. Benjamin, also a very strong visual learner, uses daily graphic organizers but Lucia hadn't considered using them with Danika or Maxine. Maybe she should.

Tomlinson (2001) provides several strategies for understanding the needs of students who struggle: Identify students' strengths and design tasks with those in mind. Enhance their strengths instead of focusing only on remediating what they cannot do. Make what they are learning relevant and ensure they understand the key concepts or principles. Create tasks that are slightly more difficult than what you think the children can accomplish, and support them in completing them (i.e., scaffolding). Tomlinson also calls this strategy "teaching up." Provide many avenues to learning so the curriculum is accessible to everyone. Accept your students for who they are unconditionally and believe in their potential (pp. 13-14).

Deciding on appropriate assessment tasks can be difficult for teachers. Many students appear to be doing worse than they are because of the chosen assessment. This is particularly true for children with disabilities. As children progress through the primary grades, assessments often include more tasks that involve writing and memorization. Children who struggle with these are at an automatic disadvantage. It is important to keep several key things in mind while you are considering assessments:

- Provide opportunity for ongoing assessment through differentiation.
- Provide a variety of avenues through which children can demonstrate their knowledge.
- Be very clear on what you are assessing. The task should assess only the expectations you identify. Do not lump in other things (e.g., neatness, spelling, artistry, etc.) unless they are expectations you are specifically assessing. For example, if you are giving a test on habitats, you would not take off points for spelling errors. The students need to know up-front if you decide that you are going to use a science project as a way of assessing conventional grammar expectations as well as science expectations. A child who cannot write will have a modified program in the writing component of language arts (meaning she is not completing grade level expectations); this does not mean she needs modified expectations in all subject areas. Find a way, other than writing, for her to demonstrate her knowledge.
- Determine whether the expectation is foundational and requires mastery. This may lead to opportunities for multiple assessments (through varying avenues) of the same expectations.
- Be creative. Consider portfolios (online and on paper), dramatizations, oral reports, visual representations, audio- and videotaping, and peer scribes/readers.
- If a child has an IEP and requires accommodations for assessment, you *must* provide them. Incorporate choice in products or other assessment tasks so that she isn't the only one doing something different.

If you adhere to the philosophy of differentiation, you will find that any accommodations, modifications, or adaptations you need to do will not feel like extra work. They are already included in your plans, and chances are good that more than one child will benefit from the options.

### Opportunities for Play

Kindergarten generally provides many opportunities for play during a school day. Dramatic play is encouraged and many of the centers include writing materials to facilitate emergent literacy. Literacy is incorporated directly into the play activity. For example, children playing in a post office can write letters, design stamps, or make signs.

The value of play can be difficult to explain to those who adhere to more traditional methods of direct instruction. Even more difficult is trying to convince these proponents of direct teaching and drill on isolated skills that young children do not learn well this way. (Callas, Bruns-Mellinger, & King-Taylor, 1998, p. 21)

Many children with disabilities have difficulty initiating play or maintaining an activity with peers. They are included less often in interactive play than their peers without disabilities. Although degrees of social separation do seem to vary with severity of disability, even children with mild disabilities are less accepted as playmates than those children without disabilities (Diamond & Stacey, 2000, p. 63; as cited in Mastrangelo & Killoran, in press). Inclusion can play an important role in creating equitable play situations. Proponents of inclusion believe that it is vital to encourage social interactions between children with disabilities and their peers. Lucia thinks of Benjamin. Although he interacts well with his peers, he only does so when she puts him in a group. She has not yet seen him initiate play with his peers, and many of his peers don't know what to make of the PCS that he uses. Lucia hasn't spent enough time teaching the class about the pictures and their meaning. There's no point in having Benjamin use a PCS if Lucia is the only other person who communicates with him while using it.

The teacher becomes a very important person in this equation of play and inclusion, since she has the power to break down the barriers facing children with disabilities (e.g., inadequate materials, lack of opportunities to play with peers, inaccessible toys in the environment, etc.) (Mastrangelo & Killoran, in press). Some of the ways to eliminate these barriers include providing environmental support, adapting materials, simplifying the play activity by reducing the number of procedural steps, using child preferences, and providing special equipment/assistive technology, adult support, peer support, and "invisible" support through naturally occurring events to increase the probability of a child's success (Sandall, 2004).

For typically developing children, learning through outdoor play experiences comes easily and naturally. Outdoor play may make children with disabilities even more socially isolated, however (Flynn & Kieff, 2002). As children enter the later primary grades, their play can become quite physical; rough and tumble play peaks at this stage of development (Papalia, Olds, & Feldman, 2002). Children like Maxine or Raymond may have difficulty controlling their movements and may hurt a peer unintentionally.

During this age span, children move towards playing games with rules (Bredekamp & Copple, 1997). At first, the rules seem quite arbitrary and are made up by the children. They become quite industrious at ensuring that everyone follows the rules. By the 3rd grade, many children are able to play games with complex rules. Children with disabilities may be at a disadvantage here. Teachers who creatively team peers and suggest adaptations to the materials, or changes to the rules, set the example that everyone is included in play.

Before inclusion can happen, teachers must want to do it and believe they can do it. With the right mindset, frequent collaboration, and effective teaching strategies, teachers can create a welcoming, challenging, and supportive environment for all children. Including children with disabilities into the kindergarten and primary general education classrooms can become a reality for all teachers. Successful inclusive experiences in these classrooms will create a foundation for children with disabilities and their families—a foundation upon which they can build a lifetime of learning experiences with their peers in their community schools.

## Notes:

[1] Accommodations for ADHD would require a Section 504 plan in the United States, unless there was a co-morbid learning disability or behavioral expectation. Although ADHD is not recognized as an exceptionality in Ontario, accommodations can be given without needing an identification.

[2] In Canada, some provinces refer to these documents as personal program plans (PPP), individual support service plans (ISSP), or individual program plans (IPP).

[3] "Expert or distinguished teaching focuses on the understandings and skills of a discipline, causes students to wrestle with profound ideas, calls on students to use what they learn in important ways, helps students organize and make sense of ideas and information and aids students in connecting the classroom with a wider world (Brandt, 1998; Danielson, 1996; Schlechty, 1997; Wiggens & McTighe, 1998)" (Tomlinson, 2000, p. 7).

## References

Bredekamp, S., & Copple, C. (Eds.). (1997). *Developmentally appropriate practice in early childhood programs* (Rev. ed.). Washington, DC: National Association for the Education of Young Children.

Callas, J., Bruns-Mellinger, M., & King-Taylor, M. (1998). Play. In E. A. Tertell, S. M. Klein, & J. L. Jewett (Eds.), *When teachers reflect: Journeys toward effective, inclusive practice* (pp. 1-36). Washington, DC: National Association for the Education of Young Children.

Canadian Ministry of Education and Training. (1998). *The Ontario curriculum, grades 1-8: Science and technology*. Toronto, ON: Author.

Diamond, K. E., & Stacey, S. (2000). The other children at preschool: Experiences of typically developing children in inclusive programs. In S. Sandall & M. Ostrosky (Eds.), *Natural environments and inclusion*. Young Exceptional Children, Monograph Series 2 (pp. 59-68). Longmont, CO: Sopris West.

Flynn, L., & Kieff, J. (2002). Including everyone in outdoor play. *Young Children, 57*(3), 20-26.

Gartrell, D. (2004). Misbehavior or mistaken behavior. In D. Gartrell, *The power of guidance: Teaching social-emotional skills in early childhood classrooms* (pp. 6-18). Clifton Park, NJ: Delmar Learning.

Katz, L. G., & Chard, S. C. (2000). *Engaging children's minds: The Project Approach* (2nd ed.). Westport, CT: Ablex Publishing.

Mastrangelo, S., & Killoran, I. (in press). Play and the child with disabilities. In C. Ferguson & E. Dettore (Eds.), *To play or not to play: Is it really a question?* Olney, MD: Association for Childhood Education International.

Papalia, D., Olds, D., & Feldman, R. (2002). *A child's world: Infancy through adolescence* (9th ed.). Boston: McGraw-Hill.

Sandall, S. R. (2004). Play modifications for children with disabilities. In D. Koralek (Ed.), *Spotlight on young children and play* (pp. 44-45). Washington, DC: National Association for the Education of Young Children.

Tomlinson, C. (2000). How to differentiate instruction. *Educational Leadership, 58*(1), 6-11.

Tomlinson, C. (2001). *How to differentiate instruction in mixed-ability classrooms* (2nd ed.). Alexandria, VA: Association for Supervision and Curriculum Development.

## Case Study

*Lucia's students love Greta, the class guinea pig. They have been asking about other animals and what they eat and where they live. They've talked about pets, but Lucia would like to expand this interest so that it meets more of the science curriculum expectations. Specifically, she would like to cover the following expectations:*

- *Compare ways in which animals eat their food, move, and use their environment to meet their needs*
- *Describe ways in which animals respond and adapt to their environment*
- *Identify and describe behavioral characteristics that enable animals to survive (e.g., migration, dormancy, hibernation). (Canadian Ministry of Education and Training, 1998, p. 17).*

## Questions

Using the strategy of differentiation, what activities could Lucia ask the students to do and what products could they pursue? Remember to take into consideration readiness, interest, learning style, and life circumstances and experiences. For each expectation, identify three different tasks. How will you assess them?

Make sure to include the four children from the vignette as active members of the groupings.

# Chapter 5

# Junior Level, Grades 4-6, Ages 9-12

*Billie L. Friedland*

*Amanda is a 9-year-old 4th-grade student who lives in a rural, wooded small town. Amanda tests within the normal range of intelligence; however, she has been having difficulty with reading, word recognition, and word-attack skills since the end of 2nd grade, which in turn is slowing her reading rate and affecting her comprehension and writing composition. Amanda's basic math skills are at grade level, but word problems give her trouble due to the level of required reading involved. Amanda has glasses for mild amblyopia, but she sometimes forgets to wear her glasses to school.*

*Background information reveals that Amanda had been born cord-wrapped and was anoxic at birth for 5 to 6 minutes. She was bagged with oxygen immediately after birth. Her Apgar scores were low but within normal limits. When Amanda was 4 years old, she had slight tremors during the early morning wake-up period, but none were noted at other times of the day. She was never observed to have a noticeable seizure episode. Amanda's father is a construction worker for a local contractor, and her mother is a nurse who is currently on medical leave. Amanda spent her preschool years at home or in child care when both parents were working. Amanda's mother reported that Amanda had difficult tantrum behaviors during her preschool years; in response, her parents used loss of privilege or time out. Amanda is calmer now and strives to please adults. She exhibits no behavior problems in school, other than a tendency to become frustrated with reading tasks and a tendency to be off-task and to give up trying during problem solving.*

Every child deserves a safe and supportive learning environment. Assuming that a goal of education is to build inclusive communities in which all citizens participate and make valued contributions, then accommodation, adaptation, and assistive technology (AT) supports are for everyone, when and where they are needed. For example, someone carrying an armload of books might use a hip to hit the pressure plate that triggers the door in a public building to open automatically. Would you say that this is an unacceptable use of an environmental accommodation? I doubt it. Accommodations and adaptations can be helpful to all students and are worth teachers' time and effort (Vaughn, Bos, & Schumm, 2003).

Today, however, many educators feel hard-pressed when they try to put into practice the premise that accommodations are for everyone. First, they find that it bumps up against traditionally enculturated teacher ideas about treating every student in the instructional setting equally. Second, many think that most students can meet the learning standards without any accommodations.

Some students need accommodations, modifications, and adaptations because they have a specific disability that hinders or impedes learning in some way, while others come to the learning situation with different cultural or ethnic backgrounds and/or with language-related differences, such as learning English as a second language. Students who have difficulty finding the correct words or understanding the nuances of language have problems establishing meaning (semantics) (Friend, 2005). In addition to this diversity, individual learning preferences also play a role. Some students process information from one sensual modality better than from others (Friend & Cook, 2003). For example, some are better at visual learning, while others learn better from hearing words or sounds. Indeed, this is why teachers are encouraged to use multi-modal instruction and assessment (Rose & Meyer, 2000).

Students' needs for support are further compounded by the changes brought on by technology. Technological changes have affected each of us, regardless of our abilities. Seelman (1998) listed some of these changes, as follows:

- Rising use of the Internet for information exchange
- Increasing use of computers in schools and the workplace
- Increased techno-awareness and demand on the part of persons with disabilities, their families, and advocacy networks
- Recent legislation and litigation regarding the need for assistive technology and other supports
- Decentralization of program administration, from federal to state levels
- New expectations for persons with disabilities
- The need for individualized and systems technologies to be integrated, synchronous, and complementary.

The effects of these changes on junior level students, grades 4 through 6, are critical and profound, both because of the students' developmental period, and because of their increased need to synthesize tremendous amounts of information. According to Piaget's later works, the concrete operational child "de-centers" her or his attention, allowing for new cognitive processes to occur, such as conservation (i.e., the child's ability to recognize sameness, or knowing that equivalence between two sets or substances remains the same despite alterations in physical arrangement or conditions of containment). To accomplish this, the child attends to relevant dimensions and uses this information in several ways to develop notions of reciprocity, compensation, irreversibility, and negation (Ginsburg & Opper, 1988). These are essential foundations for the higher order thinking skills that are required in classroom and school-wide assessment. As curriculum demands increase, the academic performance of students who are not adequately supported for learning in general education classrooms at this level tends to fall further and further behind that of their peers. In turn, this has a negative effect on their self-esteem and social relationships in terms of peer acceptance (Vaughn, Bos, & Schumm, 2003).

The need for information/communication access is most urgent in junior level settings. Without accommodation, adaptation, and AT in the classroom, Internet and multimedia will remain inaccessible for some students (Bender & Bender, 1996). Furthermore, without attention to accessibility and usability in the classroom, these students will not have full access to the curriculum. Consequently, accommodations and adaptations in educational classrooms and settings should amount to doing whatever it takes to ensure that all students have the opportunity to participate as fully as possible in the general curriculum and, ultimately, to earn a diploma (Beech, 2003a). This chapter presents accommodations, adaptations, and AT supports as they relate to various areas of instruction and assessment. Consider the case of Amanda while reading the chapter.

## Assessing Individual Strengths, Needs, Interests, and Preferences (SNIP)

### Academic Performance and Progress

For years, many legislators and educators erroneously believed that children with disabilities would not be able to meet the goals and standards set for their peers. Consequently, these children were often excluded from the curriculum and large-scale testing. This attitude has begun to change. For example, current federal legislation in the United States explicitly mandates that educational goals and standards apply to all students. The Educate America: Goals 2000 Act (U.S. Senate, 1993), Improving America's Schools Act of 1999, and Individuals With Disabilities Education Act (IDEA, 2004) require districts to report on the performance and progress of all students, including those with disabilities. This is becoming common in other countries as well. Teachers have developed standards and ways of assessing the extent to which students meet established standards. Concurrently, because of widespread technological changes, students today need a higher level and more complex set of skills. Therefore, they require considerably more focused and intensive schooling than did students in past generations (Salvia & Ysseldyke, 2004). In addition, the student population is more diverse in terms of background, experiences, and readiness.

For all these reasons, it is imperative that assessment data be meaningful and accurate. It is in the junior grades, or just before, that large-scale assessments, with high stakes, often begin. Salvia and Ysseldyke (2004) note five factors that can affect the accuracy of assessment: 1) student understanding of assessment stimuli, 2) response to assessment stimuli, 3) nature of the norm group for comparison, 4) appropriateness of test items, and 5) individual students' exposure to the content being assessed. Unless accommodations are made during testing, assessment practice runs the risk of discriminating against students with disabilities and at-risk students if their disabilities or risk factors should prevent them from responding in ways that can be meaningfully evaluated.

While it is well-known by practitioners in the education field that all students need additional supports from time to time, under current U.S. education laws, only students with documented disabilities or those who are English language learners are allowed to receive accommodations of any kind. This is not the case throughout Canada. In Ontario, for example, accommodations can be made for children who are not identified and/or do not have an IEP (referred to as ISSP, IPPP, or PPP in other provinces). However, until very recently, province-wide assessment accommodations had to be included on an IEP in Ontario if they were to be granted. Currently, a school's principal can make decisions on an individual basis.

Major categories in which most states and provinces[1] allow accommodations for tests are: 1) presentation of directions and testing materials, 2) response modes, 3) scheduling, 4) setting, and 5) assistive technology. Some examples include, but are not limited to, the following: enlarging print, magnifying or amplifying materials, translating oral directions into sign language, providing symbols on tests or answer sheets to help clarify directions, reading directions aloud, rereading or explaining directions, providing printed directions, reading the test to the student (unless the test is in reading), providing text-to-speech technology, allowing the student to read the test aloud to himself as he works, making color transparency layovers to enhance visual perception, providing white noise, giving verbal encouragement, and underlining or highlighting key words. If a child needs an accommodation for a large-scale assessment, then the child also will need accommodations for classroom tests.

For classroom tests, teachers can group similar items, arrange easier items first, provide a word bank for fill-in-the-blank items, eliminate one of the choices in multiple choice items, select fewer questions that measure the objectives aligned with standards, grade separately for mechanics and content, and allow students to use notes or a textbook for reference (unless memorization is required).

Multi-modal assessment is key to understanding the strengths and needs of the student, so changing the response mode is essential (Council for Exceptional Children, 2004). For example, students can answer oral questions, write an essay, solve a problem, create a skit, or map out a concept. Teachers can increase space allowed for answers. Students can tape-record answers, dictate to a proctor or aide, sign responses, respond in Braille, word process or type answers, write on test protocol, or use color-coded lines. For mathematics assessment, students can use grid paper for alignment of computation; use an abacus, calculator, or multiplicative grid; and use alternative or augmentative communication devices for responding.

### Assessing Instructional Needs

Standard diagnostic and curriculum-based assessments continue to provide the most usable, specific information for teachers about what students need to learn in relation to what knowledge and skill clusters should be further developed. Criteria-based measures, such

---

**Possible Test Accommodations**

Enlarged print
Magnified or amplified materials
Sign language interpretation of oral directions
Provide symbols on tests or answer sheets to help clarify directions
Read directions aloud
Reread or explain directions
Provide printed directions
Read test to the student (unless the test is in reading)
Provide text-to-speech technology
Allow student to read test aloud to self as she works
Make color transparency overlays to enhance visual perception
Provide white noise
Give verbal encouragement
Underline or highlight key words
Provide a scribe
Give extended time
Provide frequent breaks

as those used in state- and province-wide testing programs, simply identify the standard indicators that are met or not met at a given grade level at the time of a particular testing session. The purpose of this testing is to determine what the students know and can do at their grade level. Out-of-level testing may be necessary in some diagnostic and instructional decision-making situations.[2]

## Diversity Considerations

Since the 1960s, research has indicated that factors associated with poverty and differing expectations between home and school settings have a negative impact on students' academic achievement (Bloom, 1982). The challenge for educators is to ensure that a greater number of students with disabilities, or from diverse backgrounds and family situations, have equal opportunities to receive the best education possible.

Some common characteristics of diverse learners concerning language usage have emerged from the literature. For example, poor readers use contextal cues more than good readers do for word recognition, whereas good readers use contextal cues more for comprehension and extension (Kame'enui, Carnine, Dixon, Simmons, & Coyne, 2002). First, organization of information for retention is based on individual experience and perception, and thus is bound to be different for students from diverse backgrounds. Second, the relationship between working memory and organization is unclear and requires further study. Finally, learners with diverse needs name objects less quickly than average achievers. These are truly language-related issues, since diverse learners and average achievers do equally well on recalling nonsense syllables (Kame'enui et al., 2002). This finding has implications for addressing both organizational and memory skills, suggesting that students need opportunities to actively use the new information through activities that focus on rehearsal and categorization and that emphasize meaning. Such activities strengthen both short-term recall and long-term memory. Teachers can help students with memory difficulties to enhance reading comprehension by providing procedural facilitators, such as story maps, study guides, and inquiry guides. In addition, Wong (1991) indicated that diverse learners have difficulty applying learning strategies, and had more difficulty adjusting to structure and in making transitions from less to more successful strategies. Teachers must teach students how to use learning strategies effectively, give examples of when to use and when not to use a particular strategy, and require mastery of using each step within a strategy.

Another consideration for children of diverse backgrounds is phonological awareness and the sheer number of words they must learn to define and store. A strong relationship exists between phonological awareness and reading acquisition (Kame'enui et al., 2002). Therefore, any activities teachers can do to improve language coding strengthens phonetic storage and the ease with which students learn to read.

## Interests and Preferences

There is nothing so disheartening as to meet adults with disabilities who still do not know their own strengths, needs, interests, and preferences. To achieve their potential, students must be taught early to manage their own learning strategies and coping mechanisms. The period spanning 4th grade through 6th grade is a perfect time to begin this process. According to Elliott and Thurlow (2001), teachers can take several steps to help students identify the accommodations and adaptations that are needed for classroom instruction and tests. Such steps include the following:

- Ask the student about what helps her or him learn better.
- Ask parents about what they do at home to help the child complete tasks and homework assignments.
- Record the students' strengths and needs in areas linked to curriculum.
- Identify the prerequisite skills necessary for acquisition of new learning.
- Teach students the best ways to use their accommodations and/or adaptations.
- Determine if the accommodation is being used effectively.
- Promote and encourage the use of the accommodation.
- Systematically collect data and track the use and effectiveness of the accommodation or adaptation, so that data-based decisions can be made about justification in relation to need and effect.
- Teach the student to reflect on his or her strengths, needs, interests, and preferences.

## Self-determination and Self-advocacy

Students need to develop self-determination, knowledge, and skills. They need to assert their preferences, express their needs and desires, and develop as much self-sufficiency as they will need for adult living. They must begin early to develop skills at choice-making and decision-making. Moreover, they must learn to work with others to collectively advocate for their own needs and the needs of others. These are critical self-determination skills for all students. The I-Plan self-advocacy strategy is one way to help develop their choice-making and self-advocacy strategies (see Van Reusen, Bos, Schumaker, & Deshler, 1994; Wehmeyer, 1995, for details). What better way for students to learn the value of self-determination than to be integrally involved in their own IEP process (Vaughn, Bos, & Schumm, 2003)?

## Accommodations

The bottom line is that accommodations must not compromise the essential requirements of the program. According to Deschenes, Ebeling, and Sprague (1995), teachers need to ask some general questions when deciding whether accommodations are needed: "How can the individual student successfully acquire the desired knowledge and skills? Do schedule and practice opportunities need to be changed to address the individual rate of progress that the student is making? Does the individual student require more feedback and encouragement? Can the student manage independent work as well as his peers?"

Classroom management techniques, such as rotating class leadership, allowing everyone to help out in some way, providing signals for impending transitions, bringing activities to closure in a meaningful and orderly way, and giving students opportunities to have a say in class rules are all techniques that promote student ownership in the routine and structure of their classroom, thereby promoting student cooperation.

Instructional techniques should follow well-established procedures, such as using advance organizers, cue words, or symbols to highlight important information, frequently repeating important information, offering both written and verbal presentations, numbering ideas, putting difficult words on the board, and using pictures, diagrams, or semantic mapping to show linkages and relationships. Above all, model expected behaviors, because teacher behaviors are key to successful instruction and management of the learning environment. Teacher behaviors can even compensate for adverse conditions, such as overcrowded classrooms (Robinson & Friedland, 2004).

Most teachers are already making maximum use of common technology, such as tape recorders, self-timers, communication devices, word processors, and overhead projectors. Some computer-assisted programs, primarily in the areas of math and reading, are programmed to provide selected activities based on a child's previous responses. Testing accommodations done through the computer medium have been shown to raise test scores (Rose & Dolan, 2005).

Integrating technology into curriculum is a bit more complex for students in junior level grades because of their developmental level and need to synthesize larger bodies of information. Students with special needs and diverse backgrounds particularly need to be taught strategies (Carnine, as cited in Kame'enui et al., 2002)—general steps to problem-solving or analyzing content. Strategies help students learn such higher order thinking skills as problem solving, decision-making, and critical analysis and synthesis. Therefore, technology used in the classroom should be purposefully selected to support instructional and learning strategies. In choosing software, teachers should look for minimal clutter and distraction. Directions need to be clear and concise. The student should be allowed to go back and correct errors, save work, then exit and re-enter the program easily. Teachers should be able to use the program to consider requisites and provide adequate review.

## Developing Academic Support Skills

### Personal Development

All students should be encouraged to share their hobbies, extracurricular interests, and skills with peers in the classroom. Today, more students are being educated away from the mainstream—in magnet schools, in private schools, or at home. The effect is largely a brain drain on the mainstream of public education. Students lose out on having classmates with particular backgrounds and interests, and schools lack parent support. Having peer models who are comfortable sharing their interests and talents with students is an invaluable medium for informal learning and a facilitator of interest and motivation.

### Communication

Many children with disabilities or from diverse backgrounds have difficulty learning, because they lack the necessary communication skills to acquire information basic to forming concepts or developing skills in curriculum areas. If a child does not often initiate conversation or does not know how to formulate or ask questions, then these skills must be specifically taught. Children need to develop a certain comfort level with talking in a group, describing observations, asking questions, and cooperating to problem solve or create a group project. Furthermore, students must be taught observation, inquiry, and discovery. They must learn how to report, both in group and out of group. They must task-out activities and partner with other students to complete tasks.

### Health and Emotional Well-being

Many children require accommodations and adaptations because of conditions and circumstances beyond their control. For example, in one 5th-grade class in the midwestern United States, a young girl would come to school late and fall asleep in class almost every day. The teacher always had her particular lessons and materials prepared in advance, making time, when the child awoke, to present her with information, give assignment directions, and arrange for assignment completion. When I questioned the teacher about why she was bending over backwards for this child, the teacher responded by saying, "Don't ask. You don't want to know. I am working with our school psychologist to support this child because there are things going on in that home that should not be happening." The teacher did not know at the time that I was the neighbor directly behind and across the alley from the house where the little girl lived. The lights were on all night and people came and went at all hours. It was not until after the police cracked down on the family's operation that I found out they were making methamphetamine in the kitchen and selling it out the back door all night long. This child and her small brother never had adequate rest at home, and many of their other needs went unmet.

Teachers also need to work with students in inclusive classrooms on their acceptance of racial, cultural, and individual differences. This must be systematically done, both on the whole-group and individual level. Conflict resolution, role-play, effective speaking, listening, and helping skills; empathy training; values clarification; and leadership skills are essential components.

By the end of the junior grades, students should be participating in community organizations and activities. This is the time to learn about democratic processes and civic duties. Volunteering, fund-raising, surveying, and shadowing adults who participate in community advocacy are but a few ideas for involving students in the community.

## Career Awareness

Junior level students need to begin sorting out what they might like to do when they grow up. Career awareness begins in infancy when babies start to develop notions of adult roles. Students need exposure to a variety of traditional and non-traditional careers. Schools can host Career Days, as they are a good way to bring in community persons who can talk about, and demonstrate aspects of, their careers. Another good method is having students shadow adults for a day at their jobs and then report their findings back to the class. Career tours can be arranged collaboratively with area business and industry spokespersons, government representatives, or human service professionals. Adult friends and neighbors are good sources for one-on-one dialogues about career expectations and rewards. The progression from career awareness to career exploration to career preparedness must be made as smoothly as possible. Collaboration among professionals, parents, and community representatives is key.

## Home and Family

Home and family activities, issues, and concerns are important to talk about in school, because school offers an emotional distance and objectivity not usually afforded within the family. Students need to learn about home safety, caregiving, parenting, child development, financial management, food handling, medical records, and much more (Beech, 2003b). Academic units or learning centers can be developed around the most critical of these topics.

## Creative Thinking and Productivity

Knowing when and how to provide hints, cues, and prompts is crucial to developing creative thinking and spurring students on to higher order thinking. This is a skill that teachers develop over time and with experience working with students. It is related to the counseling skill of knowing when to engage and when to withdraw from conversing with a client. Teachers can drop hints to jog a student's memory of previously learned information, while cues and prompts should motivate further inquiry into linkages and relationships that lead to discovery. Teachers can accomplish much the same effect by judiciously selecting instructional tools and materials that provide similar cues, prompts, and hints. Students must learn to understand, choose, and integrate strategies as well. If students are expected to engage in problem-solving situations, they must be able to not only apply strategies, but also know when not to apply certain strategies (Kame'enui et al., 2002).

Students need encouragement to persist in problem solving or creative activities until an acceptable solution is worked out. Persistence is often instrumental to success. Students also need to learn that progress is never a straight line forward—they will hit snags. How to work through snags is part of the creative and learning process.

## Organization and Study Skills

Study guides are tools that can help a student through a reading assignment by directing the student's attention to the key points. Study guides also provide structure for the student's reflection on what she is reading, thereby developing higher order thinking (Vaughn, Bos, & Schumm, 2003). Some publishers provide commercially prepared study guides to accompany the textbooks. While study guides can be real time savers, be aware that the publisher does not know your style of teaching or your students' individual needs. Study guides are particularly useful for students who have difficulty maintaining focus. Some study guides help students to identify patterns, establish linkages, and determine meaning. Students also need to learn test-taking skills (Deshler & Schumaker, 1986) and such study skills as managing their time and routines, organizing notes, using mnemonic memory strategies, systematically reviewing, creating flashcards, and learning what is expected on the test.

## Personal Assistance and Self-determination

Some students with disabilities have paraprofessional or medical assistants who remain in the general education classroom throughout the day. For most, this is essential support. However, by some accounts, there are drawbacks. Teacher education students who have observed in classrooms during their early field experiences have reflected that, at times, it appears that having an aide in the classroom prevents students with disabilities from interacting informally with other students. The aides often respond on those students' behalf, resulting in the students' social exclusion. If an aide modifies instruction or assessment in ways that deny the child access to the curriculum that is taught to his peers, then it can have a devastating impact on the student's self-esteem and the development of self-determination skills. Teachers must ensure that students receive only as much support as needed and that the child and aide do not become a class unto themselves.

The junior level age range is one of great growth. Peers become more central and teachers must consider the social impact of their efforts. With appropriate accommodations, modifications, and adaptations, students will be able to negotiate through these years successfully.

## Notes:
[1] Canada has 10 provinces and three territories. It is understood that when the word "province" is used, it could also refer to one of the three territories.

[2] NCLB allows for alternate assessments for children with disabilities, although there are conditions on how results are counted (Overview of No Child Left Behind Act of 2001).

## References

Beech, M. (2003a). *Accommodations: Assisting students with disabilities. A guide for educators.* Tallahassee, FL: Florida Department of Education, Bureau of Instructional Support and Community Services.

Beech, M. (2003b). *Accommodations and modifications: What parents need to know.* Tallahassee, FL: Florida Department of Education, Bureau of Instructional Support and Community Services.

Bender, R. L., & Bender, W. N. (1996). *Computer-assisted instruction for students at risk for ADHD, mild disabilities, or academic problems.* Needham Heights, MA: Allyn and Bacon.

Bloom, B. (1982). *Human characteristics and school learning.* New York: McGraw-Hill.

Council for Exceptional Children (CEC). (2004). *The new IDEA: CEC's summary of significant issues.* [Online] Available at www.cec.sped.org

Deschenes, C., Ebeling, D. G., & Sprague, J. (1995). *Adapting curriculum and instruction in inclusive classrooms.* Bloomington, IN: Institute for the Study of Developmental Disabilities, The Center for School and Community Integration.

Deshler, D. D., & Schumaker, J. B. (1986). *The learning strategies curriculum.* Lawrence, KS: Edge Enterprises.

Elliott, J. L., & Thurlow, M. L. (2001). *Improving test performance of students with disabilities: On district and state assessments.* Thousand Oaks, CA: Corwin Press.

Friend, M. (2005). *Special education: Contemporary perspectives for school professionals.* Boston: Pearson.

Friend, M., & Cook, L. (2003). *Interactions: Collaboration skills for school professionals* (4th ed.). Boston: Pearson.

Ginsburg, H. P., & Opper, S. (1988). *Piaget's theory of intellectual development.* Englewood Cliffs, NJ: Prentice Hall.

Individuals With Disabilities Education Act of 1997, PL 105-17; and the new IDEA 2004 [Online] Available at www.ed.gov/Offices/OSERS/IDEA/the_law.html

Kame'enui, E. J., Carnine, D. W., Dixon, R. C., Simmons, D. C., & Coyne, M. D. (2002). *Effective teaching strategies that accommodate diverse learners* (2nd ed.). Upper Saddle River, NJ: Merrill Prentice Hall.

Robinson, A., & Friedland, B. L. (2004, March). *Encouraging students to reflect on their early field experiences across two semesters.* Presented at the 24th annual American Conference on Rural Special Education, Orlando, FL.

Rose, D., & Dolan, B. (2005). *Assessment and universal design for learning.* Center for Applied Special Technology (CAST) Associate Editor Column. Journal of Special Education Technology [Online] Available at http://jset.unlv.edu/15.1/aseds/rose/html

Rose, D., & Meyer, A. (2000). *Universal design for learning.* Center for Applied Special Technology (CAST) Associate Editor Column. Journal of Special Education Technology [Online] Available at http://jset.unlv.edu/15.4/asseds/rose.html

Salvia, J. & Ysseldyke, J. (2004). *Assessment: In special and inclusive education* (9th ed.). Boston: Houghton Mifflin.

Seelman, K. D. (1998). *Blueprint for the millennium: An analysis of regional hearings on assistive technology for people with disabilities.* Prepared for the National Institute on Disability and Rehabilitative Research (NIRDD). U.S. Department of Education, Office of Special Education and Rehabilitative Services by United Cerebral Palsy Associations, Washington, DC.

Overview of No Child Left Behind Act of 2001. 20 U.S.C. 6301ei.seq. (2002). [Online] Available at www.nochildleftbehind.gov/next/overview/index.html

Van Reusen, A. K., & Bos, C. S. (1990). I-PLAN: Helping students communicate in planning conferences. *Teaching Exceptional Children, 22*(4), 30-32.

Van Reusen, A. K., Bos, C. S., Schumaker, J. B., & Deshler, D. P. (1994). *The self advocacy strategies for educational and transtion planning.* Lawrence, KS: Edge Enterprises.

Vaughn, S., Bos, C. S., & Schumm, J. S. (2003). *Teaching exceptional, diverse, and at-risk students in the general education classroom.* Boston: Pearson.

U. S. Senate. (1993). Goals 2000: Educate America Act, S. 1150, 103rd Congress, 1st session.

Wehmeyer, M. L. (1995). *Whose future is it anyway?: A student-directed transition planning process.* Arlington, TX: The ARC of the United States.

Wong, B. Y. (1991). The relevance of meta-cognition to learning disabilities. In B. Y. Wong (Ed.), *Learning about learning disabilities* (pp. 231-258). Orlando, FL: Academic Press.

## Case Study

*Amanda's teacher and mother met to discuss Amanda's progress. Amanda's father could not attend, as he was working. Together, they discussed Amanda's reading and problem-solving difficulties, including Amanda's inability to sustain attention to task details. They decided which steps each would take. Amanda's mother scheduled another eye exam to determine if further correction was required. None was noted, but the mother promised to check each morning to make sure Amanda was wearing her glasses to school. She also scheduled a medical appointment to check on Amanda's current health status and get advice about nutrition. The teacher made a contract with Amanda that established reinforcers for Amanda wearing her glasses in school. The teacher conferred with the Child Study Team (CST), which conferred with the school psychologist, who scheduled an evaluation of Amanda with the neuropsychologist. When that process was complete, Amanda was diagnosed as having ADHD without impulsivity, and so she was prescribed a mild stimulant.*

*In the classroom, the teacher planned and implemented several strategies for improving Amanda's word recognition and word attack skills. These strategies involved help with phonetic organization, vocabulary meaning and linkages, and composition on the computer. The teacher began making study guides for reading assignments that helped Amanda and several other students in the class to identify main points and structure the relationships among topics. Now, Amanda is contributing to group problem-solving activities and seems to be happier in school. Her math grades are slowly improving. She is reading more and comprehending more. Her mother is pleased that her grades have come up in both areas by one letter grade.*

## Questions

1. How can Amanda successfully navigate the 4th-grade curriculum? Do schedule and practice opportunities need to be redesigned? Does Amanda need more systematic feedback and encouragement? Can Amanda manage independent work? What specific support does Amanda need? How can Amanda contribute to and benefit from the classroom social environment? What instructional techniques and best practice procedures will benefit Amanda? What can Amanda's parents do at home to accommodate Amanda's learning?

2. What environmental or social accommodations can be made to help Amanda obtain the necessary resources and complete assignments? Will assistive or adaptive technology tools be needed?

3. How well does Amanda manage changes in routine and transitions from one activity or setting to another? Will the instructional and assessment organization require accommodations to support Amanda's individual need for structure and focus?

4. Can Amanda use the same kind of books, tools, materials, and instructional resources as other 4th-grade students?

5. What knowledge and skills are critical for successful learning and eventual transition to adult living?

# Chapter 6

# Middle School/ Intermediate Level, Grades 7 and 8, Ages 12-14

*Lucia Schroeder*

*Ms. Martin's 8th-grade history class of 30 students is hard at work. Quiet? No. Well behaved, actively involved? Yes. Homogeneous? No. One look reveals the broad range of the students' physical development, from short to tall, slim to overweight, fragile to muscular, nearly shaved heads to long black hair highlighted with hot pink. Intellectual, social, and emotional development are equally diverse at this dynamic age level.*

*A closer look reveals students with exceptional qualities and special needs. Aleah recently arrived from Somalia via a refugee camp. Although she converses with her classmates fairly well in English, her grasp of educational English is at a beginning level. Maria is bilingual—fluent in Spanish and English—and she loves the challenge of debate and music. Her family has strong ties to its Hispanic heritage. Peter is constantly in motion. Chatting easily with his classmates, he is more comfortable in the gym than in the classroom. Tim moves slowly, looks neither happy nor sad, and settles into his assigned seat with a simple "Hi" to others at his table. He sometimes stays for afterschool study club, but does not participate in sports or other student activities. He needs extra time in order to learn. The students disperse throughout the room to their assigned tables. Some slide quickly into chairs, while others make a production of squirming into their chairs. As friends separate, the noise level drops.*

*Ms. Martin begins the lesson with a fast-paced current events discussion. She calls first on Tim, a student who struggles academically and is receiving specialized help. As Ms. Martin usually does, she asks if anyone can add to Tim's comments, then calls on several other students to add to his event or share another. Her segue to the day's topic is to ask for connections between current events and the information they are finding in their project work.*

*The topic is early civilizations. Students gather into six smaller groups, each studying a different civilization in a different part of the world. To introduce inquiry as the learning strategy for this unit, Ms. Martin showed the class key terms they might encounter. She puts these words on mini-posters, using large print, and hangs them on the classroom walls, adding a few terms each day. She asks volunteers to create drawings for the key terms. Ms. Martin reminds the* students that they should discuss their findings among themselves and record them in their logs at the end of the class period. Each group has questions to answer about their area of inquiry as they prepare their class presentations. They must include a map of the continent, a reference to foods, job differentiation, and a model of housing or another structure.

Available resources include coloring books, travel posters, videos, textbooks, hard copy encyclopedias, and access to online sources. Today, Ms. Martin draws students' attention to the four classroom computers beside Mr. Dean, a paraprofessional. He explains that his role for today is to assist anyone who needs help finding information by using online virtual tours or other computer-based sources. Students have previously learned and practiced skills for teamwork. Ms. Martin provides students with a checklist so they know her expectations and that both process and product will be assessed.

Aleah is working on the map for the earliest civilization in central Africa. A teammate assists with naming rivers and geological features by pointing them out on the textbook map. After the teammate says the names, Aleah repeats the words and copies them neatly onto the map. Maria is working on Mexico and assists by easily reading names of people and places and adding some comments that are based on her personal experiences. Another student reads aloud from a text source as his group tries to rephrase the material into adolescent language. Tim shares a computer printout of information he found on China during his study time. When asked by his teammates, he tells them about the main idea of his findings. He makes suggestions for the model his team is making for its presentation. Peter stands by the resource table as he selects an issue of National Geographic and a travel brochure, then returns to his group to explain his findings.

Each student is actively engaged. Ms. Martin circulates through the room, answering questions—usually by asking them back with a new twist or suggesting an easily understood resource. When groups have trouble working together, she asks the students about the problem and reminds them to work it through as though they were a council. By suggesting appropriate resources, Ms. Martin provides encouragement. She assists with difficult words or concepts. She encourages students who are restless to move around the room. She checks on supplies and resources.

Mr. Dean assists at the computer station, offering help to anyone who needs it. He also watches Tim and Peter for signs of frustration and heads in their direction when needed. He gives an 8-minute warning so students can complete their paragraph or activity by the end of class time. Two minutes later, he gives another reminder for students to return all resources to their storage area so the next class can find them. At that point, students write in their logs to indicate what they learned during this class. The teachers most want to see which key ideas and sources of information the students have produced, although sketches and descriptions may be added. Aleah uses the print-rich classroom to help with her writing. Peter draws a diagram and labels it.

During the presentations that follow the inquiry process, the maps and models are displayed around the room. A guided discussion will accentuate the similarities in the early civilizations and challenge students to make connections to civilizations today. A large Venn diagram will be created to record the discussion. Student understanding of these generalizations will be assessed by a carefully written multiple-choice test. A study guide will be given to those who need it. Ms. Martin and Mr. Dean have carefully planned the unit to provide all students with positive and informative learning experiences that provide a challenge without causing frustrations. They have included social, emotional, and intellectual learning objectives and experiences.

The goal of this chapter is to provide ideas for enhancing learning in inclusive, middle/intermediate level classrooms. Suggestions are included for enabling all students in the general education classroom. Students at this age are changing rapidly, as their bodies are in various stages of puberty, their minds are bombarded with information in and out of school, and their emotions may become volatile. Most students covet peer acceptance. Vygotsky's (1986) theories of scaffolding through social interaction and of a zone of proximal development provide a basis for many of the suggestions that follow. The previous vignette provides a reference point. When modified slightly, these ideas can be applied to other class settings.

In the vignette, Ms. Martin begins class with current events as part of a developed routine. By calling on Tim first, she helps him take part, because no one else will have already reported on his topic. Each day she will begin with a different student. Shy students or those who have difficulty accessing current events will be among the first called upon, and Ms. Martin will have alerted them the previous day. She spends time visiting with students, so she is sensitive to their needs and abilities.

Special education teachers and paraprofessionals help Tim and Aleah share their events during homeroom at the beginning of the day to refresh their memories and help them give clear summaries. At this middle age level, the specialists are careful to create an "I can!" attitude among the students rather than conveying an "I'll help you" expectation. Previewing lessons and pre-teaching vocabulary are crucial to achieving this goal.

As Ms. Martin moves the students into the day's lesson, she segues from current events to past history. She reiterates the overall unit goal and the lesson objectives for the day. She encourages students to be mentally and physically engaged in her classroom activities.

### Involving Students and Activating Their Prior Knowledge

Having a standard opening routine helps students activate the history/social studies portion of their brains and thus transition into this class from their previous class. During this time, the learning objectives for the day are introduced—a helpful strategy for students like Tim who need structure for learning.

In any classroom, a pleasant teacher who models enthusiasm for the subject has far-reaching effects. Facts and concepts are remembered longer and with more understanding when the teacher is cheerful and has a positive attitude. As Claudia Cornett (2004) says, "That worth remembering is learned with enjoyment." Every adult in the classroom needs to exhibit a positive attitude and a belief that all students can learn. For students of this age, the term "child" is a put-down. "Student" is preferred, and "teen" is usually a compliment.

Student involvement is another dimension of attitude. Middle school teacher Rick Wormeli (2001) encourages teachers to use the following techniques for getting students to invest in lessons:

- Express interest in knowing and being with your students
- Create an emotionally safe environment [lead by example; model, model, model]
- Use stories [appropriate student stories rank first; teacher-shared stories, next]
- Offer vivid lessons [occasionally dress up, bring props, provide mnemonics]

- Express enthusiasm for your subject [body language and voice must match]
- Build suspense [give sneak previews with words and/or objects]
- Maintain momentum [the beginning and end of class are best remembered]
- Use games. (pp. 8-15)

An exemplary teacher goes beyond modeling and holds high expectations that students will be able to meet the standards set before them. A pervasive "You are capable, you can do it" attitude is essential in working with all 12- to 14-year-old students, since their lives tend to move in waves rather than ripples. Strong self-confidence allows them to ride out the low troughs.

It is no secret that activating prior knowledge more effectively leads to learning. Whatever method is chosen—anticipatory set, K-W-L, or attention grabber—the effective teacher seeks to activate the class-related memory stored in each student's brain. For students with special needs, including those with language difficulty, learning challenges, or an inability to sit still and/or concentrate, awakening their prior knowledge is a critical component of effective teaching and learning. An education specialist who knows students well can help each student determine the best method he needs to use. Effective activities may include drawing a logo in their student planners, displaying a "code word" as he enters the classroom, or using a hand signal.

Allington (2002) cites extensive research that indicates three to five minutes as adequate for activating previous learning. Ms. Martin achieves this goal in her classroom through the ongoing use of current events and a summary of the goals for the unit. Ms. Martin or Mr. Dean might start with a cartoon, song, ballad, poem, dialogue, or a short reading related to the topic of the day. Realia, or strong visuals, are vividly explained and shared with all of the students via computer or overhead projection. Students who struggle with literacy especially need something tangible to see or touch. Establishing learning teams that require students to physically move is another means of drawing their attention to the current task. Movement helps all students learn better but is essential to students like Peter, who has an attention problem with behavioral concerns. For him, physical movement helps to center his thoughts on the learning task.

Ms. Martin refers to the small groups as teams. She spent time early in the year using sports analogies, modeling, and practice to teach students that a team interacts and makes the best use of every player's capabilities as they work together. Team members depend on each other; they question each other and work together to solve problems. This is what makes them a team, rather than simply a group (Fink, 2004). As teams studying an ancient civilization, they are reminded to use the talents of all players and to depend on each other for help. Mr. Dean and Ms. Martin shared in modeling and teaching this problem-solving approach to learning.

**Discourse**
The vignette also highlighted the discourse of the subject and previews of pertinent vocabulary. The discourse of a subject is the way that people talk, read, or write about a particular subject (Buehl, 2001). Discourse with a medical doctor or grandparent is different than with a friend. The sudden silence that happens when a respected adult enters a room full of teens exemplifies this idea, as teens change from peer chatting to

adult-oriented discourse.

A study of history may involve the use of time lines, maps, diagrams, or other reference materials. Rivers may be discussed as means of transportation as well as sources of water for drinking, feeding animals, and irrigating crops. Such terms as "trade," "regroup," "colony," "balance," or "period" may have different meanings than they do in math, science, or English class. Social studies has multiple themes and standards. Consequently, the discourse may vary from course to course. For example, the discourse of economics—using such terms as "hedge," "stock," and "latitude"—may differ from that of geography. Personnel working with students with special needs are more effective if they teach the unique qualities of a subject's discourse through pre-teaching, repetition, and examples from students' experiences and review. It is important that all personnel have a common understanding of the discourse in each discipline in order to avoid confusing students.

In effective inclusive classrooms, the teacher develops student awareness of the discourse used in the class. As middle school and junior high students move from room to room and teacher to teacher, distinctions among and between subject matter discourses are vital for student success. If students write one or a few key words for each subject in their planners at the beginning of the day, they may have an easier time transitioning between classes.

Wilkerson and Wilkerson (2004) highly value the need for teaching socially appropriate discourse to students with Asperger's syndrome. They use the term "social savvy" to describe the process of distinguishing between acceptable hallway discourse, as peers move *between* classes (e.g., locker talk), and what is acceptable *in* the classroom. This process does not come naturally for the student with Asperger's syndrome, a "neurological condition marked by a significant impairment in social interaction" (Wilkerson & Wilkerson, 2004, p. 19). All teens benefit from understanding the "what and why" of socially appropriate discourse at school, and those with Asperger's syndrome particularly need guided learning. Social competence helps balance the difficulties faced by students with physical, emotional, or intellectual challenges. As students reach puberty, with all its physical and social changes, this life stage calls for renewed learning and modeling of appropriate behavior.

### Teamwork
The concept of teamwork is closely related to the above description of social savvy. Opportunities to model and practice team skills in small groups will help students develop skills for contributing information to the classroom team. Accepting ideas from others and working together to produce a product are skills that need to be taught and practiced, rather than simply assuming that all students at this age level have mastered them (Carmean & Haefner, 2002). These students are in various levels of developing independence and interdependence. Learning to give and take is valuable, and receiving recognition both for small and large contributions is important for progress. The social part of the social studies class is extremely valuable to preteens—more valuable than memorizing historical data.

### Critical Vocabulary
In an effective class, students learn the vocabulary of the topic and how to use various comprehension strategies. Students at the intermediate/middle level need assistance transferring reading skills from one class to another. Summarizing strategies learned in literature class will need to be repeated as comprehension strategies for social studies class.

The vignette demonstrated how a word wall of key terms could help students learn vocabulary and understand the sources they studied. Ideally, both students and teachers will add terms that are new or unfamiliar in meaning and that appear to be significant for understanding. Teachers can introduce key terms early in the inquiry process. Realia, paired with key terms, is the strongest conveyer of vocabulary. Realia in this unit might include unprocessed foods, outdoor grilled foods, soil samples (such as heavy clay), or reeds and grasses for weaving. Using pictures and virtual tours of historic sites is a practical way to explore civilization. For larger concepts (such as political systems), improvisational drama, dance, or discussion may add to student understanding. The emphasis needs to be on key terms, not on obscure, seldom-used words.

To thoroughly understand information, vocabulary lessons are essential before, during, and after reading. Pre-study of selected critical terms is especially valuable. For example, "civilization," a broad concept, may need to be studied in several ways, while knowing the name of a river or an ancient king may not. Students studying civilization might learn concepts by using Frayer's Model to examine examples and non-examples of a civilization (Graves & Graves, 2003, p. 92); by discussing the root word, "civil," and the meaning of its affixes (Greene, 1998); and, as the final presentations are made, by noting the similarities and differences among the reports. Teachers of students like Aleah, Tim, and Peter will need to use knowledge of each student's abilities and interests to determine the critical terms for the students to master and how each will learn them. Understanding a few terms that will have future use is important.

Students who are gifted, such as Maria, need to be encouraged to explore in depth, and to acquire unique (and, to them, interesting) vocabulary. Maria might be encouraged to share her findings by adding them to the word wall, creating a short drama, or teaching them to her teammates. Learning to discern what is valuable and where to find information are lifelong learning skills.

Using Vygotsky's (1986) zone of proximal development theory as a guide, the students who read materials at their independent reading level will learn the most and with less frustration. Resources require different levels of decoding and understanding skills. For example, different parts of the brain are used to study pictures and drawings, discern real from fake information on the Internet, interpret maps and graphs, or summarize or read less familiar scripts. All students will need resources that correspond to their independent reading levels. Ms. Martin and Mr. Dean will introduce the various ways of reading the available materials. They will model such skills as noticing titles, turning headings into questions, and studying pictures and diagrams before beginning to read. Students who are less able readers may need help with these skills in and beyond this class. Some students will more easily decode travel brochures with many pictures, while others may enjoy the challenge of encyclopedia entries or a mystery novel set in ancient times.

## Comprehension Strategies

One comprehension strategy that teams can use involves questioning each other. Students learn by forming questions as well as by answering them. "What do you think this statement about calendars means?" is more likely to lead to learning than saying, "I don't get this!" Either is preferable to just pretending to understand, however. Composing the question and thinking through the answer both involve higher level thinking. Patience, guided practice, and modeling aid students in developing their ability to question. For students who struggle academically, learning to question others will be a big step, as will reframing questions until they are understood. Likewise, learning to look for answers and formulate them into words is also a brain-intensive task that can be a powerful learning tool. Emphasis on teamwork encourages this type of learning.

Because students in an inquiry team approach are working relatively independently, the teacher should incorporate whole-class and team-guided practice as they begin. In a whole-class approach, guided practice would mean having students read text together as it is projected on a screen. The teacher models her thought processes. For example, the teacher might turn the title or headline into a question, attend to graphics, or note that in news articles the most important information comes first. For reading travel brochures, she would direct students to look for examples of advertising compared to information about the historic sites. Precautions for using information from the Internet would include paying special attention to the source. Using the same word with different domain endings (i.e., ".gov," ".org," ".com," or ".net") might help them understand that sources vary in reliability and accuracy. The lead teacher of this activity would need to carefully preview the sites. During this activity, Mr. Dean might work closely with students to make sure they are following the presentation.

After the teacher presentation, all students would have an opportunity to practice the skills with peer and teacher assistance. Mr. Dean would encourage students who read more slowly by reviewing the information with them when they are at the computer or have ready access to the reading materials. A review of these skills a short time later would encourage extended memory. These strategies would apply to other classes, too.

Bringing together the team members' research makes them revisit the material and enhances their comprehension. This synthesis encourages students to use their strongest areas of intelligence. Multiple intelligences are necessary to complete this study of early civilizations. For example, students who are kinesthetic can build the model, while students with musical and interpersonal skills can use them in the presentation. Literacy skills are needed in the researching and writing phases. Newly learned vocabulary can be shared. Social skills are reinforced as team members work together on parts of the project. When students encode what they have earlier decoded, deeper understanding is developed.

Students observe each other's maps, watch and take part in the presentations, and compare their own findings to those of classmates. The emphasis needs to be on sharing information, not on judging the performance or analyzing details. The general education and special education teachers serve as planners, enablers, and coaches as well as instructors in this unit of study. They are the scribes as students look for overarching similarities in the project learning. They provide effective learning environments that enable all students to meet the course learning standards.

## Synthesizing

Student journals, observation of daily work, presentations to the class, and a multiple choice test on key concepts provide formative and summative assessment data. When the teacher uses a variety of in-class experiences, students learn to trust each other, to communicate differences without being obnoxious, and to realize that some students need more time or assistance, but all have strengths.

Teachers can use several techniques to provide effective learning environments for 12- to 14-year-olds. Activating students' prior knowledge might be done with direct statements, questionnaires, surveys, text reviews, or visual material. Student involvement in activating prior knowledge will set the stage for engaging all students in the learning process. The success of students' participation will depend on the teacher's attitude, pace of the lesson, appeal to student interests and abilities, and the time of the class. Some topics will readily lend themselves to student engagement, and some students will be more involved in the lesson because of their attitudes and learning styles.

Explain and model the discourse of the discipline. This may be done initially by creating an awareness of the discourse and continuing to model the discourse as the class progresses.

Teach unfamiliar vocabulary prior to reading, whether from printed text, a computer screen, or directions for hands-on activities. Vocabulary development is enhanced if the teacher encourages independent reading with accountability and reads aloud to students from a wide variety of texts. Reviewing new vocabulary after reading may be a further step and will increase students' comprehension.

Teach a variety of strategies that students can use to comprehend text. Strategies might be simple (such as skipping unimportant words, rereading, or reading ahead) or complex (such as note-taking, paraphrasing, outlining, or creating time lines or concept maps). A particularly complex and highly effective strategy is to have students explain information or processes to others.

Teamwork will engage students in appropriate social interactions in the classroom; however, the skills leading to teamwork must be taught, not assumed. Students in the 12- to 14-year-old age group are already coping with numerous changes in their lives. Providing assistance with appropriate interpersonal interactions will encourage overall learning.

Educators working with students with special needs help them by knowing their students' strengths and challenges, by pre-teaching essential concepts and skills, and by coaching them in appropriate peer interactions. They serve as coaches and cheerleaders, as well as resources in the general education and special education classrooms.

Cooperative learning by inquiry teams may not be the most effective teaching method for all topics. To be successful, teachers need to be comfortable with this method, and it must be a match to the topic. The strategies suggested here can be implemented in other class structures and learning environments. As Lucy Calkins (1991) said, "Good teaching comes not from the quantity of good ideas, but from the way those ideas fit together into a dramatically satisfying whole" (p. 128). In the effective classroom, all students learn and develop intellectually, emotionally, and socially in a friendly, enjoyable atmosphere.

## References

Allington, R. L. (2002). What I've learned about effective reading instruction from a decade of studying exemplary elementary classroom teachers. *Phi Delta Kappan, 83*(10), 740-747.

Buehl, D. (2001). *Classroom strategies for interactive learning.* Newark, DE: International Reading Association.

Calkins, L. M. (1991). *Living between the lines.* Portsmouth, NH: Heinemann.

Carmean, C., & Haefner, J. (2002, November/December). Mind over matter. Transforming course management systems into effective learning environments. *EDUCAUSE: Review, 37*(6),

26-34.

Cornett, C. (2004, October). *Learning through laughter.* Presentation at E-3 Education Conference, Eastern Illinois University, Charleston, IL.

Fink, L. D. (2004, September). *Want your students to learn more? Some new ideas for designing your courses differently.* Workshop at Eastern Illinois University, Charleston, IL.

Graves, M. F., & Graves, B. B. (2003). *Scaffolding reading experiences: Designs for student success* (2nd ed.). Norwood, MA: Christopher Gordon.

Greene, J. F. (1998). Another chance: Help for older students with limited literacy. *American Educator, 22*(1& 2), 74-79.

Vygotsky, L. S. (1986). *Thought and language.* Cambridge, MA: MIT Press.

Wilkerson, C. L., & Wilkerson, J. M. (2004). Teaching social savvy to students with Asperger's syndrome. *Middle School Journal, 36*(1), 18-24.

Wormeli, R. (2001). *Meet me in the middle: Becoming an accomplished middle-level teacher.* Portland, ME: Stenhouse and Westerville, OH: National Middle School Association.

## Case Study

*Ms. Martin's approach to the civilization unit is a good example of differentiation (as discussed in Chapter 4). Consider the following scenario: You are assigned to co-teach 30 students in an inclusive grade 8 science class. There are individual texts for each topic—outer space, earth science, and biological sciences. For this term, you are studying earth science.*

*You have three children with intellectual disabilities in your class: one has a hearing impairment and several students have various levels of attention problems with behavioral concerns. Two students are English language learners and you suspect another is struggling but does not want it known. As the general education teacher, you would like to brainstorm with the special education resource teacher for ideas to enable all students to learn and enjoy science.*

### Questions

Thinking about content, process, product, readiness, learning style, and interests, answer the following:

1. How could you engage students in their learning process?

2. What methods could you use to assess your students' prior knowledge?

3. How would you explain and teach the discourse of science to these 14-year-olds?

4. What environmental/instructional accommodations or curriculum modifications might allow these students to work more cooperatively with each other?

5. How would you know if the students have effectively met the objectives?

# Chapter 7

# The Secondary Level, Grades 9-12, Ages 14+

*Lynn Walz and Angela Pitamber*

*George lives with his mother and stepfather, but spends his summers with his father. George has received special education support since the end of 3rd grade. He performs at the 10th percentile on national group achievement tests. As George enters the 9th grade, he is reading at the 4th-grade level; he knows how to calculate all operations for whole numbers, but not fractions or decimals; and he can generally write a simple sentence, but his writing often contains misspelled words and incorrect punctuation. He has beginning keyboarding skills and uses the Internet at home for entertainment and personal communication. Throughout the middle grades, George continued to improve his basic skills through group instruction provided at his instructional level. In the summer, he works with his father on construction projects. During the school year, his main entertainment is the local skateboard park. He learns skateboard tricks on a weekly basis by watching others at the park. Most of his friendships with peers are confined to school; even at the park, he often skates alone. Although George gets along well enough with his family, there seems to be little evidence that the adults at home spend much time with him or provide support for success at school. Most of their energy is spent trying to make ends meet financially.*

*Alexandra has difficulty with short-term memory and organizational skills. She is reserved and seldom asks others for assistance. She generally does what is expected in classes but often turns in her assignments late or not at all; consequently, her grades are low. Alexandra was adopted and moved to this country at the age of 3 after living with a group of children on the streets of her home country. Little is known about her original family and early life. In her new country, Alexandra was enrolled in preschool programs and quickly learned to speak the new language. Her academic skills are within the low normal range; she performs at the 30th percentile nationally. Although a medical history is lacking, it is assumed Alexandra has neurological damage caused by genetics, a birth defect, or as a result of early malnutrition. She uses social cues to follow classroom activities but has few positive peer interactions. Her family is able to provide the financial and emotional support needed.*

Secondary education is the springboard for adult life. In the secondary setting, students begin to make their own decisions about courses to study. Secondary students make elective course selections for a variety of reasons: social, career, recreational, personal fulfillment, and sometimes even educational. They consider what classes their friends are taking, what courses will best prepare them for work or postsecondary education, what courses will be fun and provide knowledge about their personal interests or hobbies, and what courses will help them become well-rounded and competent persons in society.

Course selection and the connection to adult outcomes are critical to successful and productive secondary education. Course selection and successful completion will result in three positive outcomes: 1) transition to the adult world, 2) meeting the requirements for a secondary diploma, and 3) recognition of self, leading to the sense of personal advocacy necessary for self-determination. Consider the vignettes as we begin the discussion of accommodations, adaptations, and modifications at the secondary level.

Both of these students are in the process of moving from dependence to independence. Both students will benefit from the support of others in school and at home. Both students will address the issues associated with transition to adulthood, meeting the requirements of earning a diploma from the secondary school system, and achieving positive self-advocacy as a result of personal articulation of their strengths and weaknesses.

## Model for Problem Solving

Determining the need for, selection of, and effective implementation of accommodations, adaptations, and modifications is most effectively and efficiently done through a problem-solving model (Fuchs & Fuchs, 1987; Graden, Casey, & Christenson, 1985; Shinn, Habedank, & Baker, 1993). A variety of models can be found. One of the most simple is the 15-minute Problem Solving Model by Randall Sprick (1987). An elaborate model is Collaborative Planning, designed by Together We're Better (Thurlow et al., 1999). All research-based models for education problem solving have the common elements of problem identification, intervention design, and program evaluation.

Problem identification begins by listing all the education concerns. The educator also identifies current instructional practices, curriculum expectations, and environment or learner strengths. Focus is given to one problem, or a small group of related problems. This problem (or problem group) is clearly articulated through data gathered by review of documents, interviews, and observations in the natural setting and by formal or informal test results. A clear articulation of the problem and current strengths is the critical first step to designing effective interventions.

Intervention design generally begins by determining if an accommodation or modification is needed. Accommodations are supports that result in the student achieving the expectation of the environment, such as using a tape-recorded textbook to learn concepts, having tests read aloud, allowing a student to use a voice-sensitive computer to complete written assignments, or changing an assignment from essay to multiple choice. Modifications are an alteration of the curriculum expectations for a student—for example, expecting the student to identify the safety rules in a kitchen rather than read and follow the recipe independently, or expecting the student to say three meaningful comments during class discussion rather than write a summary of the points of view presented by the class. The vast majority of students with disabilities will benefit from an accommodation. Few students need modifications.

Designing an effective intervention is most successful when there is a clear connection to the identified problem, the current strengths are utilized, and a hypothesis states the specific assumed reason for the problem. For example, one might assume from reading the case studies at the beginning of this chapter that George is failing a class because he does not accurately read the textbook, while Alexandra may be failing because she loses her assignments before she can complete them. The problems are clearly different, requiring different interventions.

Designing an intervention also includes determining how that intervention will occur. Intervention selection begins by identifying the resource available, investigating scientifically effective strategies (evidence-based) or techniques, and considering simplicity of application. Generally, the best starting point is with interventions that cost the least in time and money, are related to the problem, and are supported by research. For example, the number one way to improve a skill is to use that skill. The most effective way to improve reading is to read. So, an effective intervention for improved reading is to allow a student time to read materials at his level and establish a system that includes personal accountability and incentives for doing the task. Provide a student with a book that he can read during study hall or before bedtime and reward him for each book completed. If the student reads 3 to 5 times per week, he will likely improve his reading skills. This does not mean that a student should spend a lot of time practicing skills that are difficult. Students need to experience success. Most of their time should be spent using their strengths to meet the curriculum expectations.

The final element in effective education problem solving is intervention evaluation. Did the intervention solve the problem? To make this determination, you must collect data that relates to the problem and the desired outcome. Has the student submitted more assignments? Is the student becoming a more fluent reader? Are more points earned for classroom assignments and tests? Is the student following class safety rules independently? Data can be collected in a variety of ways. Some examples of data collection are: sampling behavior (e.g., the student's oral reading rate for one minute), anecdotal reporting (teacher says, "Yes, more work has been submitted"), or observation (checklist for safety). When one problem is resolved through an intervention, the same approach can be used for other problems.

## Transition to the Adult World

The primary goal of secondary education is preparing students for the adult world. The next step after secondary education may be further education or training, employment, or working toward growing independence. Whatever the choices students make, secondary education is preparation for the future.

For our purposes, transition refers to an adolescent whose lifestyle is transformed from the role of a student to the responsibilities of an adult. The transition from school to independent adult life is difficult for many adolescents, particularly those with disabilities. Studies have shown that students with disabilities do not receive the necessary assistance in transition planning (DeStefano & Wagner, 1993; Peraino, 1992). In order to assist in this process, students will require support from various sources, such as family, friends, school administrators, and community agencies. Adolescents with disabilities will need access to the necessary aids available. As an adult, the student will have to be concerned with issues of employment, postsecondary education, independent living, leisure, and community participation.

## Jobs and Job Training

Although the majority of students who have a learning disability will enter the workforce, they will face immense competition. Consequently, educators need to provide students with the important skills required in different fields. Students must be aware of their interests and capabilities, and also have teachers and parents show them the steps that will help them get a job. An example of a program that can help students decide on a desired field is the "co-op" program, which also provides students with much-needed job experience (Brown, 2000; Gerber & Brown, 1997).

## Postsecondary Education

Following secondary education, many students with disabilities will learn a trade through a vocational school or apprenticeship program. Although the percentage of students with disabilities who continue on to college or postsecondary education is on the rise, more students could be prepared for this option. Students who receive the information and training necessary to make this type of decision would be more inclined to consider postsecondary education as a realistic option (Stewart & Lillie, 1995). Colleges and universities are expected to provide students with reasonable accommodations and address their individual needs, as students may encounter a complexity of concerns not experienced throughout high school.

Many transition programs attempt to connect employers with students with disabilities, giving the students employment opportunities that cater to their skills. Thus, students can move with ease from high school to full employment without the fear of entering the wider job market. With adequate planning in high school and the necessary supports, the transition from one stage of life to another should occur with greater ease.

## Home and Independent Living

As students' homes are their primary environment, their experiences there and the support they receive can either help or hinder their learning. A supportive family can help a child with a disability accept and understand his particular disability, as well as develop coping strategies. As much as the family can affect the life of the adolescent with a disability, the adolescent likewise affects the lives of those he lives with (Turnbull & Turnbull, 1996). A strong family unit can aid the child with emotional support and assist with issues in learning. Conversely, a family unit that is unable to adapt to the diverse needs of the adolescent can cause great problems for him. It is important that parents or guardians not only provide support where needed, but also recognize ways in which they can help their child become independent and responsible for his own life.

## Recreation and Leisure

Social interactions and relationships outside of the home can provide an increasing awareness of the world and foster growth for a student with a disability. Students with a disability usually find themselves isolated in a society that they do not fully understand or are unable to integrate into. Particular social behaviors may become difficult to comprehend, which can adversely affect their education (Janney & Snell, 2000). One excellent way to address this problem is an intervention called Circle of Friends. To understand the Circle of Friends, envision four circles extending out from the child: a circle of intimacy, a circle of friendship, a circle of participation, and a circle of exchange (Forest, Pearpoint, & O'Brien, 2000; Killoran, 2002). By filling the inner circles with friends and supports, the quality of the person's life will improve. Circle of Friends is a proactive approach that involves searching out peers, schoolmates, and community members who can make a difference (Killoran, 2002).

## Community Participation and Access

Collaboration between parents and educators is very important in the transition process for a young adult. It is necessary for parents to work alongside their child as well as their child's teacher when making decisions about their child's future. When parents believe that they have a role in deciding their child's future, they feel more connected to their school and become supporters of their child's right to an education (Ferguson, Ferguson, & Jones, 1988; Hanley-Maxwell, Whitney-Thomas, & Pogoloff, 1995).

Work placement programs also can help students with a disability gain access to the workforce in a manner that caters to their learning. Educators, parents, and the community need to work together in order to ensure a successful transition for students. More programs also need to be implemented at the postsecondary level to encourage students to continue their education after high school. With sufficient support in place, the student will come to see that there can be a full life offered to him once he completes his secondary education.

## Class Selection

Inclusion becomes more difficult at the secondary level and requires teamwork between the content-area teacher and the special education resource teacher. They need to work together in order to prepare lessons for students in the general education class. Together, they can create strategies to assist students with learning difficulties as well as to help set up a learning plan that will best meet the students' needs. According to Deshler, Schumaker, Harris, and Graham (2000), students need greater services to be provided for them at the secondary level, particularly when deciding which courses they should take. It is important for parents, teachers, and students to work hand-in-hand when deciding which courses would be most beneficial for a particular student. When making such decisions, it is essential to envision possibilities for the student after high school so that the courses will provide the skills needed for gainful employment and furthering the student's education.

## Cooperative Education: Transition From School to Work

In cooperative education, students are exposed to and begin to learn the skills required to obtain and keep a job. One model of a cooperative education program entails a semester course in which students spend one month in the classroom learning about how to be employable individuals (e.g., learning about résumés, dress codes, behaviors, interview manners and questions, responsibilities, etc.). For the other four months (the rest of the semester), students are either placed in or find their own job. Both the employer and the teacher complete evaluations throughout the time; the student has to have a successful evaluation in order to pass the course. Often, more than one opportunity exists for a co-operative placement in high school, allowing students to make contacts that may help in their job searching after graduation.

## Alternate Education Programs: Non-degree Postsecondary Programs

Adolescents who are unable to participate in college or work programs, but still require postsecondary transition programs, can take courses in some colleges that will allow them to learn basic skills. Such courses might include learning about independence, computers, budgeting, work/life experiences, etc. Unfortunately, not enough such programs are offered to these students to help them to survive in the real world. The goal of a non-degree program is to enable students to experience a form of college life, which is modified to meet different levels of learning.

## Requirements for Earning a Diploma

Having made the case that secondary education is preparation for adult life, our focus now will shift to meeting the requirements for a secondary education diploma and creating accommodations or modifications to facilitate that goal for students with disabilities. Most nations have established a standard for earning a diploma from secondary school (Bolt, Krentz, & Thurlow, 2002; Thompson, Blount, & Thurlow, 2002; Thurlow, Wiley, & Bielinski, 2003; Ysseldyke et al., 1998). Tests, such as college entrance tests, work readiness tests, and armed services aptitude, are often used to determine future placement for education or employment. A growing number of nations are using tests as a minimum requirement for earning a diploma.

Some professionals and families advocate that students with disabilities should be exempt from such requirements (Vitello, 1988). However, there is value, to both the system and the individual, in engaging students with disabilities as part of the standard system. Separate systems can never be equal. Students with disabilities would be further segregated by limited exposure to knowledge from a segregated system.

In the United States, testing is used to determine eligibility for a diploma at the secondary level (North Central Regional Educational Laboratory [NCREL], 2002). Students in Ontario, Canada, must pass a 10th-grade literacy test (or course if the test is failed) before they can receive a diploma. Including students with disabilities in this requirement has three potentially positive effects:

- Ensuring equality for all students at the national level (assuming there is a national standard)
- Ensuring uniform standard accountability at the regional level
- Ensuring fair allocation of resources to improve the learning of all students at the local level.

Although all students are expected to participate in high-stakes testing, the level or type of participation may vary for students with disabilities. Some students with disabilities will participate in the standard testing with no accommodations and meet the expected requirement. Many students with disabilities can fully participate and meet the expectations of the tests if accommodations are provided that do not compromise the integrity of the test (Elliot, Thurlow, Ysseldyke, & Erickson, 1997). Test accommodations can be provided for the material presentation, test setting, or allotted time (see Chapter 6 for examples of accommodations). Some students with a disability may participate in the testing with or without accommodations and have a modification in their personal standard, which reflects consideration of the identified disability for each individual. For example, the individual education plan may state that the student is required to earn fewer points on the test to be eligible for a diploma. As few as 1 to 3 percent of students (Olson, Mead, & Payne, 2002; Thurlow et al., 1999) will have no skill for the test and be exempt; however, even those students should be accounted for in the secondary system through alternate means of assessment, such as a checklist of skills attained, individual assessment tools that match personal education goals, personal performance documentation, anecdotal records of progress over time, or portfolio assessment using a collection of exemplary products. Participation in required testing, use of accommodations, or modification from the standard and exemptions are usually indicated in the student's individual education plan (this practice varies by country and province).

The assumption that all learners with and without disabilities are expected to achieve the standards set for earning a diploma should prompt educators to apply scientifically supported techniques to improve the skills of all learners. The problem-solving model is needed to design and implement effective accommodations when a student is not gaining the skills needed to earn a diploma. For example, if a student has not passed the minimal tests required to earn a diploma, additional, informal assessment data would be used to identify the skills needed to pass the required tests. If George did not pass a reading test required to earn a diploma, he could be eligible for an intervention. In this case, an intervention might involve providing direct instruction in a group with others who did not pass the test, since George's teachers know that his reading skills improved in the middle grades through group instruction. Administration of informal decoding tests might show that George is not solid in predicted vowel sounds, so scientifically supported effective methods of instruction, such as Corrective Reading Decoding (Englemann, 2002) or Rewards (Archer, Gleason, & Vachon, 2000), would be used. In this example, an intervention is provided before testing to increase a student's chances of earning the diploma.

Course requirements for earning a diploma also may require accommodations. An individual education plan can be the vehicle for clearly stating the credit requirements for a particular student with disabilities. For example, if three years of mathematics instruction are required for a diploma, one student might take courses in algebra, trigonometry, and statistics, while another might enroll in applied math for carpentry, consumer mathematics, and bookkeeping. In both cases, the students might benefit from accommodations, such as the use of a calculator, peer tutors to help them read the textbook or the tests, or student partners to assist with note-taking.

## Empowerment and Self-Advocacy

The third area of needed program development for secondary students with disabilities is empowerment through self-advocacy. Of course, students will begin the process of self-awareness before secondary education, but the teen years are a prime time to promote the skills needed for self-advocacy. Adults with disabilities are expected by most government systems to know and articulate their personal needs to secure services. Services provided to adults with disabilities often require an application to the program and self-monitoring of those services to continually meet the individual's unique needs. Training for such personal management can begin in the secondary program as the student learns to identify and request needed accommodations, with the support and mentoring of education professionals.

Self-awareness that leads to self-advocacy begins with identifying the disability and the personal effects of that disability for the individual. A student needs to learn to say, "I have a learning disability and have difficulty reading and understanding print. May I have tests read to me?" Or, "I take medication for seizures; if I have a seizure, I may fall to the floor, but do not worry. Move furniture from my head and let me have time to finish the seizure. When the seizure is finished, I will be tired and need to rest for a few hours." The more specifically the student can identify the effects of the disability, the more confident he or she will be when requesting the needed support. An amazing number of students entering high school do not know the name of their disability, although they do understand what skills they do not possess. This lack of information can lead to feelings of inferiority or shame, thereby reducing their ability to self-advocate. Students with disabilities may need one-to-one conferencing to educate them about their disability and help them identify the needed supports. The special education case manager or resource teacher is one of the best people to provide this training, either during private meetings or at the education planning meeting.

Secondary students with disabilities can become prepared for adult self-advocacy by creating a personal portfolio and practicing talking about the information therein. Some of the information contained in the personal portfolio could include education evaluation summary reports, current and past individual education plans, examples of academic work, career interest and aptitude inventories, school transcripts, and pertinent medical records. The secondary student should practice naming the items in his portfolio and describing what the information says about him. All this information is needed to justify the need for support to gain increased independence. Although this work could be accomplished in a futures planning class, few secondary schools offer this type of class to all students. Creating a personal portfolio to use in the transition to the adult world may be done as a private project with the special education case manager, resource teacher, or the student's parents.

Once the student is aware of his disability and the impact on his performance, it is time to practice self-advocacy in the secondary setting. The special education case manager or resource teacher may initially speak for the student to the content-area teacher about a useful accommodation, but the ultimate goal for the secondary student is to speak for himself. For example, the teachers might plan that the student can have all tests read aloud, but the student will approach the content-area teacher before each test to confirm that arrangements have been made to have the test read. As each semester begins, the student can be coached and prompted to talk with each teacher to review the accommodations that will be useful in that class, such as note-takers, recorded books, oral tests, special seating, and extended time on assignments. This practice in self-advocacy will be useful as the student approaches adulthood.

During the secondary school years, the student and family must become aware of the services for adults with disabilities. Services for adults with disabilities are varied and can be offered through government or private agencies. All agencies that provide support services for adults with disabilities will have an application process. It is the adult's responsibility to identify what services might be helpful, then to apply for them. The process will require the person to identify her disability, state how the disability affects her independence, and request the supports that will contribute to greater independence. There are supports for higher education, career planning and employment, independent home living, and financial management. For example, postsecondary education institutions often provide support services for students with disabilities—sign language interpreters for those who are deaf, Braille writers who take notes for students with sight impairments, audio textbooks, individual testing stations, or test readers. Employment centers may provide training or retraining for adults with disabilities to help them achieve gainful employment. Specially designed housing grants may exist for persons with physical limitations caused by disability or disease. Self-advocacy becomes a critical skill to gain the supports needed to reach adult independence.

Providing students and families with a catalog of the services available at the local, regional, and national levels will promote timely access to these adult services. Some schools have created interagency agreements with the adult service providers to promote the connection for students and families. For example, school staff can distribute to students information about adult agencies, or a representative of the adult programs might talk to secondary students or families. A transition fair could be organized among several schools to inform students and parents about adult services. During the secondary school years, the adult service providers chosen by the family or student could participate in the education planning to ensure that the student is prepared for the transition after graduation.

Self-advocacy during the secondary school years is important to ensure that accommodations or modifications are provided in all courses; however, self-advocacy becomes increasingly important as the student transitions into the adult world. Knowing and articulating needs and requesting helpful supports to increase independence are valuable skills for a successful and fulfilling adult life.

### Finding Time for Collaboration and Problem Solving

Secondary educators are busy planning instruction for several courses, providing instruction for hundreds of students daily, and evaluating and reporting on student progress. Secondary educators also spend time communicating with parents, serving on various committees, and providing extracurricular activity leadership. How is there time for content area teachers to engage in problem solving with special educators for students with disabilities? Raywid (1993) offers three solutions. The first solution involves "purchased time." Hire substitute teachers on a regular basis to free up teachers' time for collaboration. For example, a building can have three substitutes hired once every two weeks to rotate through classrooms to free the teachers for planning together for a period or two. A substitute teacher who is knowledgeable about the education plan can work with the students with the most challenging education needs, thereby allowing teachers the time to plan for upcoming events.

Another way to create problem-solving time is through "borrowed time" (Raywid, 1993). Borrowed time is regularly scheduled time for collaboration outside of the typical school day, with compensation time offered to teachers who participate. An example could be scheduling collaboration time 15 minutes before the contract day on a weekly basis, but then allowing participating teachers to leave an hour early or arrive an hour late one day of each month.

The third alternative for finding consultation time is called "structured time," a regularly scheduled time that frees some teachers to collaborate. An example of this alternative is scheduling all teachers in a department or for a grade level with the same preparation time and using the time once a week for collaboration. Assigning a special educator to attend each department meeting to provide consultation for individual student learning problems is another example of structured time. A third example is extending each school day by a few minutes and providing early release for all students on a monthly basis, thus allowing teachers to have time for a variety of collaborations. A final example is to have regularly planned adjustments to the school day with rotating responsibility for alternate activities, thereby freeing a portion of the teaching staff for collaboration. Finding time for collaboration and problem solving is critical to successful accommodation and modification for secondary students.

## Conclusion

Secondary education has three unique concerns that may require accommodations and/or modifications. They are: the transition from school to the adult world, meeting the requirements for graduation, and supporting students to be empowered self-advocates. To effectively create accommodations, a school needs a model for problem solving that clearly identifies the problem, explores and designs effective interventions, and then evaluates when and if the intervention has been successful. An effective problem-solving team requires time, whether that time is purchased, borrowed, or structured. Most students with disabilities will benefit from personal accommodations that use their strengths to improve their performance in areas of need. Some students with disabilities will benefit from content area courses with modifications in the learning expectation. Both options require an effective problem-solving team.

## References

Archer, A., Gleason, M., & Vachon, V. (2000). *Rewards.* Longmont, CO: Sopris West.

Bolt, S., Krentz, J., & Thurlow, M. (2002). *Are we there yet? Accountability for the performance of students with disabilities. Technical report.* Minneapolis, MN: University of Minnesota, National Center on Educational Outcomes.

Brookes, H. (2000). *Behavioral support: Teachers' guides to inclusive practices.* Bethesda, MD: Woodbine House.

Brown, D. S. (2000). *Learning a living: A guide to planning your career and finding a job for people with learning disabilities, attention deficit disorder, and dyslexia.* Bethesda, MD: Woodbine House.

Deshler, D., Schumaker, J., Harris, K., & Graham, S. (1999). *Teaching every adolescent every day: Learning in diverse middle and high school classrooms.* Brookline, MA: Brookline Books.

DeStefano, L., & Wagner, M. (1993). Outcome assessment in special education: Implications for decision-making and long-term planning in vocational rehabilitation. *Career Development for Exceptional Individuals, 16,* 147-158.

Elliott, J., Thurlow, M., Ysseldyke, J., & Erickson, R. (1997). *Providing assessment accommodations for students with disabilities in state and district assessments.* Minneapolis, MN: University of Minnesota, National Center on Educational Outcomes.

Ferguson, P. M., Ferguson, D. L., & Jones, D. (1988). Generations of hope: Parental perspectives on the transitions of their children with severe retardation from school to adult life. *Journal of the Association for Persons With Severe Handicaps, 13,* 177-187.

Forest, M., Pearpoint, J., & O'Brien, J. (2000, July). Circle of friends: Not a program. *Inclusion News 2000,* p. 14. Toronto: Inclusion Press.

Fuchs, D., & Fuchs, L. (1987). *Mainstream assistance teams to accommodate difficult-to-teach students in general education.* Nashville, TN: George Peabody College, Vanderbilt University.

Gerber, P., & Brown, D. (1997). *Learning disabilities & employment.* Austin, TX: Pro-ed.

Graden, J. L., Zins, J. E., & Curtis, M. J. (1985). Implementing a prereferral intervention system: Part I. The model. *Exceptional Children, 51(5),* 377-384.

Hanley-Maxwell, C., Whitney-Thomas, J., & Pogoloff, S. M. (1995). The second shock: A qualitative study of parents' perspectives and needs during their child's transition from school to adult life. *Journal of the Association for Persons With Severe Handicaps, 20,*(1), 3-15.

Killoran, I. (2002). A road less traveled: Creating a community where each belongs. *Childhood Education, 78,* 371-377.

North Central Regional Educational Laboratory. (2002). *Understanding the No Child Left Behind Act of 2001: A quick key to reading.* Naperville, IL: Author.

Olson, B., Mead, R., & Payne, D. (2002). *A report of a standard setting method for alternate assessments for students with significant disabilities. NCEO synthesis report 47.* Minneapolis, MN: University of Minnesota, National Center on Educational Outcomes.

Peraino, J. M. (1992). Post 21 follow-up studies: How do special education graduates fare? In P. Wehman (Ed.), *Life beyond the classroom: Transition strategies for young people with disabilities* (pp. 21-70). Baltimore: Paul H. Brookes.

Raywid, M. (1993). Finding time for collaboration. *Educational Leadership, 51*(1), 30-34.

Rosner, J. (1979). *Helping children overcome learning difficulties.* New York: Walker and Company.

Shinn, M., Habedank, L., & Baker, S. (1993). Reintegration as part of a problem-solving delivery service. *Exceptionality: A Research Journal, 4*(4), 245-251.

Sprick, R. (1987). *Solving behavior problems (20 minute planning process).* Video media package. Eugene, OR: Teaching Strategies, Inc.

Stewart, A. C., & Lillie, P. (1995). *Transition planning. Beyond the classroom: Secondary education and beyond.* Cambridge: Cambridge University Press.

Thompson, S., Blount, A., & Thurlow, M. (2002). *A summary of research on the effects of test accommodations: 1999 through 2001. Technical report.* Minneapolis, MN: University of Minnesota, National Center on Educational Outcomes.

Thurlow, M., Vandercook, T., Kraljic, M., Medwetz, L., Nelson, M., Sauer, J., & Walz, L. (1999). *District partnership approach to inclusion: A qualitative evaluation of impact.* Minneapolis, MN: University of Minnesota, Institute on Community Integration.

Thurlow, M., Wiley, H., & Bielinski, J. (2003). *Going public: What the 2000-2001 reports tell us about the performance of students with disabilities. Technical report.* Minneapolis, MN: University of Minnesota, National Center on Educational Outcomes.

Turnbull, A. P., & Turnbull, H. R. (1996). *Families, professionals, and exceptionality: A special partnership* (3rd ed.). Upper Saddle River, NJ: Prentice-Hall.

Vitello, S. J. (1988). Handicapped students and competency testing. *Remedial and Special Education (RASE), 9*(5), 22-27.

Ysseldyke, J. E., Thurlow, M., Langenfeld, K., Nelson, J. R., Teelucksingh, E., & Seyfarth, A. (1998). *Educational results for students with disabilities: What do the data tell us? Technical report 23.* Minneapolis, MN: University of Minnesota, National Center on Educational Outcomes.

## Case Study

*Jackie receives her report card for the first semester and realizes that her worries have been justified—she has failed two of her classes and received a D in her other two. Jackie has difficulty not only with the content of the work in each of her classes, but also with finishing it on time. She does not understand all of the assignments and cannot keep up with the daily demands. Jackie suffered a brain injury as a result of a car accident when she was in the 6th grade. She has used a wheelchair since the accident. Once she recuperated, she was able to attend school and succeed with a lot of help from her parents. Over time, however, Jackie's intellect started to deteriorate and she found it progressively more difficult to keep up with her schoolwork. She also developed a visual complication and a speech impediment. Jackie often loses her train of thought and she frequently has trouble expressing herself. The transition to high school was especially stressful, and Jackie and her parents could no longer keep up. However, her mother insisted that since her daughter put forth so much effort in her classes, she deserved to go on to university and so she kept pushing her. Jackie is unable to deal with the pressure of figuring out transportation issues, deciding whether or not to pursue her education, and other issues as well.*

### Questions

1. What needs does Jackie have for accommodations or modifications in the areas of transition, graduation requirements, and self-advocacy?

2. Choose one of the students (from the vignette or the case study) and identify three informal assessment tools that could be used to clearly define the problem or need.

3. Identify one problem for each of the students and suggest three intervention ideas supported by education research.

4. How would you begin to implement the intervention idea?

5. How would the team know if the intervention was effective for that student?

6. How would you find time to meet as a team to identify the problem, investigate a possible intervention, design and implement the intervention, and determine the intervention's effectiveness?

# Chapter 8

# Postsecondary Education: Issues of Accessibility

*Karen Swartz and Neita Israelite*

*Mark has a physical disability that affects the muscles throughout his body. He also has some functional learning challenges in his perceptual, organizational, and visual motor areas. Mark requires a physically accessible environment, including ramps and elevators. Because he tires easily, he must make use of a range of energy-conserving techniques. He wants to attend university to study to become a clinical psychologist.*

Making the transition to a postsecondary education can be a challenging experience for any student. Although students with disabilities experience some of the same challenges as their able-bodied peers, they also encounter additional barriers related to their physical, sensory, learning, medical, or psychiatric disability that may make the transition process even more difficult.

From a report on support for students with disabilities in Canada, the authors learned that colleges and universities across North America are legally mandated to accommodate students with disabilities in an effort to equalize the educational experience, as well as to create accessible academic, physical, and social environments (The Canadian Association of Disability Service Providers in Post-secondary Education, 1999). Yet, even with more institutions creating policies and guidelines to support these efforts, students with disabilities continue to confront systemic and attitudinal barriers that can make the transition to postsecondary education a difficult one. The following chapter addresses some of these barriers and provides prospective students with disabilities, teachers, and parents with information on what they can do to ensure a smooth transition. Throughout, we have included quotes from several students with disabilities who have been successful in their transitions to college, university, and beyond.

The first section, Preparing To Make the Transition, addresses the academic, physical, social, and emotional adjustments to living on or attending a college or university campus for the first time and explains what can be reasonably expected. The second section, Exploring Options, highlights the roles of all the individuals involved in helping students with disabilities make appropriate postsecondary decisions. Finally, in the third section, Road to Self-Advocacy: Empowerment vs. Helping, we address the important and vital role of the student with a disability in the transition process.

Students need to learn to take risks. As well, they need to learn to accept responsibility for their decisions and choices and, ultimately, take responsibility for shaping their own academic career. The empowerment model we propose encourages self-knowledge, awareness, advocacy, and independent decision-making.

It is our position that the key to a successful transition is not necessarily for students with disabilities to learn to become independent, but rather to increase their understanding of what it means to be interdependent; that is, to understand the things they can do on their own, the things they need help with, and the way to go about contacting individuals who can provide needed assistance.

## Preparing To Make the Transition

While preparing to make the transition to a postsecondary institution, students with disabilities need to carefully consider whether the academic programs offered by the college or university of their choice will meet their personal, academic, and career goals. Before students with disabilities accept an offer, they should fully explore their concerns related to academic accessibility. Most colleges and universities have academic policies and guidelines that commit them to maintaining an environment that guarantees students with disabilities full access to educational programs, activities, and facilities. Students with disabilities still must be vigilant about exploring how the programs they are interested in joining will accommodate their individual needs. It is important to contact the department prior to accepting an offer of admission to discuss these issues. Keep in mind that barriers to learning are obviously different for different disabilities; that is, a student with a learning disability would clearly have different barriers to learning than a student who is deaf. Making contact early helps institutions understand individual needs and make necessary arrangements for accommodations.

Each campus has an office or access center that provides support services to students with disabilities. Students have a responsibility to disclose their disability to the designated disability office if they need accommodation. It is the responsibility of the disability office to meet the students for at least a preliminary assessment of their needs. Students will need to provide the office with documentation regarding the functional impact of their impairment. It is important that contact with the disability office be made early on, so that support service staff can work with students to ensure that their academic needs can be met. In Canada, contact information for the disability service offices can be found on the National Educational Association of Disabled Students Web site at www.neads.ca.

Accommodations will allow each student an equal opportunity to demonstrate what he or she knows, as well as what he or she can and cannot do. No student should be disadvantaged by reason of disability. To avoid disappointment and frustration, students with disabilities need to set realistic, achievable, and manageable goals for themselves in relation to what the institution can reasonably offer.

For some students with disabilities, the social/emotional adjustment of living on a university campus can be daunting. This transition is packed with issues related to leaving home for the first time, sharing living space, preparation of meals, and being socially accepted by their non-disabled peers (Swartz, 2003). In a study of the educational experiences of women with disabilities, Sarah described her particular experience:

> The problem for me was making new living arrangements and moving to a new city, new people, and life's little frustrations. Because my parents had always been there to cushion my fall. . . . When I fell for whatever reasons, my parents had always been there. Now, they weren't there anymore. (Rollo & Swartz, 1998, p. 34)

It is important that students with disabilities who require specific accommodations, such as attendant care, accessible washrooms, and visual alarm systems, notify the institution's housing and disability offices well in advance of their arrival. When possible, students should request to see the residence facilities in advance to assess the kinds of adaptations that may be necessary to ensure access. Residence life coordinators should be informed about students and the impact of their disability. Steps should be taken to ensure that membership in that community is not limited by their disability. For example, staff and residents may need to attend inservice sessions and workshops on the effects of hearing loss in order to better understand the challenges faced by deaf or hard of hearing students. In planning such activities, it is imperative that the student with the disability be involved in the process.

Students with disabilities must explore their options thoroughly if they are to have a successful transition to the postsecondary environment. Taking control of their education by making informed decisions about college programs and accommodations will lessen their anxieties, ease their transition, and mark the beginning of a positive experience. One student, Alice, offered this observation:

> I grew up with the notion of not putting all your eggs in one basket. So I applied to several universities. I got accepted by one school, and we went down there and thought it was just too far away. I thought, "I know I'm gonna be homesick, and I know I'm going to have long distance bills and I'm going to go back and forth from home on the bus. But if nobody else accepts me, this is where I'll go." But then another university came along and it had everything I thought I needed as a student: a disability services office to advocate on my behalf, a student-run organization for students with disabilities, and also attendant care services, which I would need because my other goal was to live away from home for the first time. So it was a good fit. (Israelite & Swartz, 2004)

### Exploring Options

Many people are involved in assisting students with disabilities in their transition to postsecondary education. Guidance counselors, teachers, community advocates, students with disabilities who are already students at a college or university, and parents all have important roles to play in this process. These individuals can provide students with assistance in finding the right college or university and establishing a network of support within the postsecondary environment. Particularly important to the process is connecting with disability service providers. These individuals can make a great difference in the transition experiences of students with disabilities. Universities and colleges are communities, and meeting the right people during the transition phase is vitally important to the student experience. Therefore, setting up preliminary visits to meet the staff at the disability office (and possibly other students with disabilities) will ultimately facilitate the transition process.

A meeting with the university or college disability service provider may reduce some of the stress that students with disabilities feel and ease a student's transition into the college or university community. It gives the student with a disability an opportunity to share her concerns and provides the service provider with an opportunity to discuss how the concerns will be handled.

Students with disabilities will be asked to provide the relevant medical, learning, or psychological reports that will aid the service provider in making accommodation recommendations. These reports are kept in confidential files within the disability service office, and are only released with the student's written permission.

Service providers are committed to providing effective services to their students and responding to student needs as they arise; however, they also recognize that students must work collaboratively to ensure that requests and concerns are appropriately and effectively addressed. It is a reciprocal process that encourages students to participate in decision-making and acquire realistic expectations regarding their academic needs.

For many students with disabilities, a successful university experience is intricately tied to the notion of a reduced academic course load, something students are often reluctant to consider. Many students with disabilities need additional time to complete course readings and assignments, as well as study for exams. Taking a reduced course load should not be conflated with the academic ability or potential of the student with a disability. It simply affords them the flexibility and latitude needed to successfully complete their courses. Having the extra time to complete the degree may mean the difference between success and failure. Ellen, who recently completed her master's degree, describes how a reduced course load and other accommodations contributed to her academic success:

> In addition to having a reduced course load, I need extra time on exams and assignments. And, also, I have a little bit of a learning disability, so I have, through the years, gone to the academic writing centre, and so on. And then, when I went to do my bachelor's of social work, I found the writing services not really meeting my needs anymore. So I got connected to a tutor. That's helped tremendously and I'm still doing that today. (Swartz, 2003, p. 73)

Students with disabilities often have additional education-related expenses that can be quite costly. This is often a great concern for them and their families. As Ellen says,

> Let's say, for example, your parents cannot support you financially. How do you get the assistance you need to live independently? (Swartz, 2003, p. 16)

It is advisable to research the scholarships, bursaries, and other funding opportunities at the college or university of choice. Some states and provinces also may offer special funding. Students with disabilities should check out college, university, and governmental Web sites for information on financial support. Disability service providers at each institution should be able to advise on funding possibilities and how to access them.

## Road to Self-Advocacy:  Empowerment vs. Helping

Students with disabilities need self-advocacy skills for a successful transition to postsecondary education.  Ideally, the process of developing self-advocacy skills should begin while the students still attend high school.  It is critical for students with disabilities to be aware of their rights and how to conduct themselves responsibly.  Colleges and universities typically have student conduct policies, and they will not tolerate aggressive behavior from any student.  Students with disabilities are not exempt from such policies and they will need to learn how to assertively advocate for their needs without being aggressive.

School personnel should work closely with students with disabilities to ensure that they gain a realistic understanding of both their academic strengths and limitations, as well as what they can expect from the university and what is expected from them.  Developing self-understanding will help students set appropriate goals.  Part of this process is reflecting on their situations and thereby developing greater self-awareness.  Those students who develop a greater understanding of their own needs, the confidence to recognize their abilities as well as limitations, and set realistic academic goals, will have a better chance of enjoying their college or university experience.  Another key to becoming effective self-advocates is students learning the art of asking for what they need in an appropriate and responsible manner and working with faculty, staff, and service providers to achieve this.  Speaking up and addressing concerns as they arise and having the willingness to work out solutions to difficult situations will produce better results, especially when students are organized, plan ahead, and take the initiative to address their needs.

Peer-to-peer relationships may assist students with their transition and inclusion into the university community.  Many colleges and universities have either formal or informal peer-to-peer programs.  Online communication is becoming more acceptable, with the increasing number of students using computers to facilitate their studies.  Using the computer can play a significant role in minimizing social isolation, especially for students who are deaf or hard of hearing and those who may be more comfortable with language in textual, rather than spoken, form.  Online peer-to-peer relationships also provide opportunities for students with disabilities to learn and strengthen self-advocacy strategies.

> Paul:  Part of what helped me become more confident about advocating my needs is that I saw another deaf person advocate their needs to someone they just met very easily.  I said to myself then . . . if they can do this . . . I can do this as well.  It's also important to have role models . . . who can help teach the deaf and hard of hearing students how to advocate for their needs. (Swartz & Tocco, 2003, p. 16)

Barriers that students with disabilities may confront while attending college or university often relate to accommodations, residence life, on-campus transportation, and tutoring support, as well as the coordination of note taking, interpreting, and finding alternate exam services.  Senior students with disabilities can share their personal experiences and the strategies they used to negotiate the college/university environment.  Students with disabilities will need to know their rights and learn how to exercise them appropriately.

This is where the experience of more senior students can be particularly significant.

Getting involved in student leadership activities is another way for students with disabilities to integrate themselves into the college or university community. Many campuses have active disability student groups that are eager to recruit new members. Membership in formal student groups provides students with disabilities opportunities to make new friends and get involved in meaningful activities. Students with disabilities may find themselves joining institutional committees that are designed to address disability-related issues on campus. Such involvement also expands the social networks of students with disabilities, an extremely important factor in the overall college or university experience. College or university Web sites may include information about disability-related disability student groups. Although these groups are usually autonomous and not related to the disability support services offices, service providers can be helpful in making the initial contact for the new student.

> Anthony: I used many strategies. Basically, self-advocacy is one of them. You gotta rely on yourself. . . . I associated myself with places such as the organization of students with disabilities, such as the Disabilities Services Office, places that are on the same wavelength and people that share the same problems. I have many friends that have disabilities of all different kinds: visual impairment, mobility, whatever and I listen to people's problems, for example, and I share problems, and it's kind of like your support network. I started to realize that I'm not alone in this business. (Israelite & Swartz, 2004)

## Conclusion

Students with disabilities need strong support from parents, teachers, counselors, and other professionals as they make the transition to postsecondary education. An investment of time, research, and resources to thoroughly explore options, as well as preparation for self-advocacy and responsible decision-making, all pave the way for a successful university career.

## References

Canadian Association of Disability Service Providers in Post-secondary Education, The. (1999). *A report on support for students with disabilities in post-secondary education in Canada.* Retrieved July 7, 2005, from the World Wide Web: www.cacuss.ca/en/16-publications/details.lasso?pid=327

Israelite, N. K., & Swartz, K. L. (2004). [School-to-work transitions for students with disabilities]. Unpublished raw data.

National Educational Association of Disabled Students. Retrieved July 7, 2005, from www.neads.ca/en/

Rollo, L., & Swartz, K. L. (1998). *Women and disability: A workbook for teachers and students.* Toronto, ON: Centre for Feminist Research, York University.

Swartz, K. (2003). *Life transitions of students with disabilities revisited: Feminist approach.* Unpublished manuscript. York University, Toronto, Canada.

Swartz, K., & Tocco, A. (2003). [University students who are deaf and hard of hearing Talk Online]. Unpublished raw data.

Swartz, K. L., & Rollo, L. (Eds.). *Women and disability: A workbook for teachers and students.* Submitted to the Canadian Women Studies Journal and the Centre for Feminist Research.

# Case Study

*Mark researched his options at several universities. Then he made visits to three schools and met with faculty and service providers from the disability offices. He applied to the school of his choice and was accepted for admission the following September. The summer before classes started, Mark had an initial appointment with a service provider to determine his accommodations. The service provider conducted an assessment of Mark's learning and physical needs and reviewed his documentation. The following list of accommodations was based on medical and psychological reports, as well as Mark's own input.*

*Accommodations List:*
- *Use of a note taker and permission to have extra time to complete tests and exams*
- *Note takers recruited through the disability office*
- *Reduced course load*
- *Consideration for physical proximity to classes*
- *Access to tutorial services through the academic writing center*
- *Access to a copy of lecture notes prior to lecture*
- *Access to textbooks on tape*
- *Access to a computer to type exams.*

## Questions

1. How should Mark deal with a faculty member who refuses to give lecture notes to Mark prior to class?

2. One of Mark's professors has objected to the testing accommodations that have been recommended by his disability services counselor. If you were Mark, how would you manage this situation?

3. Mark must do a clinical practicum off-campus. He has several concerns about the placement to which he has been assigned. How might he address these concerns if he is to stay in this placement?
   a) The practicum requires an 8-hour day, once a week. Eight hours is too long for Mark to attend to a task.
   b) Transportation is unreliable. Mark must be there by 8:30 a.m., but the transportation service will only guarantee an arrival time within an hour of the requested time.
   c) The building does not have an accessible washroom.

# Chapter 9

# Transition Planning Options: Preschool to Postsecondary

*D. Michael Malone, Kimberly Roth, and Jennifer L. Horgan*

*Weeks after Julianne was born, her pediatrician noticed she had poor muscle tone and control. Julianne's parents also noticed she had poor sucking ability and that it took up to two hours for her to finish a bottle. After a few more visits to the pediatrician, Julianne was sent to a neurologist. Several visits later, Julianne's parents noticed that "cerebral palsy" was marked on the insurance encounter form, and they promptly asked the neurologist what this meant. The neurologist assured them that their child simply had developmental muscle delays, she would grow out of it, and that this was the only way the insurance company would cover the visit. Other doctors confirmed that Julianne did indeed have cerebral palsy, but the other doctors stated that she would have it for life.*

*Julianne began babbling at eight months of age and spoke her first word at one year. She continued to speak, but most of what she produced was unintelligible. Julianne was referred to a speech therapist at age 2, and her visits continued through her first year of preschool. When Julianne was still in preschool, her parents requested an evaluation by their school district because of their concern over her entering kindergarten. Julianne took several tests, including the Stanford Binet Intelligence Scale and the Peabody Picture Vocabulary Test, and scored in the mild mental retardation (a term not used in Canada) range. Representatives from the school district recommended that Julianne take an extra year of preschool; Julianne's parents agreed to do so and enrolled her for a second year. Julianne continued to show a delay in muscle and speech development, so she participated in therapy and had several surgeries throughout early childhood to help her condition.*

*Julianne began kindergarten in a morning half-day session, but within a few weeks was moved to a special education classroom in the morning and regular kindergarten in the afternoon. Although she was getting extra support, her parents were not pleased with the segregation. After the move, an IEP was put into place. After kindergarten, Julianne moved on to 1st grade, where she participated in general art, music, and gym classes. Julianne's core classes, such as reading and math, all were taught in a special education classroom. Some of Julianne's curriculum expectations (e.g., social skills) were on grade level, but most of her academic expectations were at a lower grade level.*

*The move from elementary to junior high for Julianne was relatively smooth, but included many new challenges. In order to prepare for her new school, Julianne received her schedule earlier than other students did so she could familiarize herself with the* building and her routine. Julianne also received her locker assignment early and her family provided a lock that opened with a key so she could practice that, too. Julianne went to all of her classes on her own, but she did leave before the official bell because of her instability in crowded hallways. Although her program of study included some regular subject classes, such as social studies, it was mainly made up of electives, such as gym and home economics. Julianne received her math and English instruction and any additional instruction for modified work in a supplemental class, which was much like a study hall, except for being in a designated special education classroom. Julianne's parents continued to feel the increased demands as she made her way through progressively higher levels of education, as any work that Julianne did not complete at school came home. Often, Julianne's parents had to sit down with her and go over her work or provide accommodations to the work themselves, such as tape-recording the material so that Julianne could listen to the information repeatedly.

The transition from junior high to high school yielded much of the same routine for Julianne. She received her schedule and locker assignment early and she and her family walked through her schedule several times before school began. Julianne continued to participate in electives as well as some English electives, such as a class on "Films as Literature." Although she had a supplemental class where her work was accommodated and sometimes modified, and where some individual instruction took place, Julianne's parents believed they had to push for more accommodations or continue to do it themselves.

As Julianne neared graduation, she still had not passed the 9th-grade proficiency tests. The school did not make accommodations for her specific educational needs, nor for the tests themselves. If Julianne were ever realistically expected to pass the tests, she would need extra time, an examination with content that tested the basic skills she understood, and someone reading the test to her. During Julianne's senior year, her parents found out that Julianne would not receive an official high school diploma since she had not passed the proficiency tests. Julianne was entitled to a certificate of completion; if she delayed accepting this, she could remain in the school system until she turned 22 (this age varies by country, province, etc.). Julianne's family decided to choose this route. Julianne worked with the local Board of Mental Retardation & Developmental Disabilities (MRDD), the Bureau of Vocational Rehabilitation, and Project Search, a joint work-study program between MRDD, Great Oaks Institute of Technology and Career Development, and Cincinnati Children's Hospital and Medical Center, for further job training and employment.

After an additional year in the school system, Julianne did not find the type of employment she was looking for; she is currently unemployed. She has recently been in contact with a new job coach through MRDD and has again started looking for employment.

Many of Julianne's transition activities were created and implemented by her family without support from the school. With more support from the school and better planning, Julianne might be in a different situation today. For Julianne, the failure to develop an effective post-school transition plan (including the accommodations and/or modifications to high-stakes tests) has real and continuing consequences. Although Julianne and her family will continue to plan for the future, one cannot keep from wondering if Julianne's progress would be different if she had benefited from more appropriate planning at key points in her education. Specific transition planning is a critical, yet typically underutilized support that can significantly enhance the quality of life for students with disabilities and their families.

Efforts to create effective inclusive educational programs are grounded in a variety of personnel, administrative, curricular, and student/family issues that require sincere, thoughtful, and serious consideration. The development, implementation, and evaluation of transition plans that facilitate grade-level promotions can represent a thread connecting these issues. Despite the developmental and functional importance of transition planning, this aspect of inclusive educational programming has received relatively limited attention and, as a result, is the exception rather than the rule (Bohan-Baker & Little, 2002; Meisels, 1999; Pianta & Cox, 1998; Pianta, Rimm-Kaufman, & Cox, 1999; Schumacher, 1998; Shore, 1998).

As Julianne's story highlights, effective grade-level transitions are not serendipitous. Not only do we need to be aware of and understand all that is related to the process of such transitions, we also need to intentionally act upon that knowledge. Transition planning and implementation can facilitate the actualization of a relatively seamless system of educational supports for all students at risk for, or experiencing, disabilities who are included in general education classrooms. In this chapter, we will offer a definition of grade-level transitions, provide an overview of what we know from transition research, present some transition essentials, outline how transition plans support basic human needs, discuss factors associated with specific transition points, and offer recommendations for effective transition planning.

## Definition of Transition

The term "transition" is defined in the Merriam-Webster online dictionary as "a: passage from one state, stage, subject, or place to another: change. b: a movement, development, or evolution from one form, stage, or style to another"; the American Heritage Dictionary of the English Language defines transition as "[t]he process of or an instance of changing from one form, state, activity, or place to another" (p. 1460). These conventional definitions of the term "transition" provide a solid foundation for the more specific use of the term in educational contexts. More formally, Kagan and Neuman (1998) defined grade-level transitions as "the manifestation of the developmental principles of continuity, that is, creating pedagogical, curricular, and/or disciplinary approaches that transcend, and continue between, programs" (p. 1). Drawing upon the preceding definitions and that provided under the Individuals With Disabilities Education Improvements Act (2004), grade-level transition can be defined as:

> A process encompassing the preparation for grade-level promotions, the interim between grade levels, and the post-promotion follow-up during which students and families experience changes in individual abilities and skills, educational philosophies and expectations, curricular organization, and physical settings and environments.

Depending on individual student and family needs, grade-level transitions can be considered grade-to-grade, or at critical junctures marked by relatively substantive, qualitative changes across grade levels (e.g., preschool to kindergarten; kindergarten to primary grades; primary grades to junior/intermediate grades; intermediate grades to secondary grades).

While grade-level transitions include physical movement from one educational setting to the next, they are much more than that. As Julianne's case shows, students can be (and typically are) readily moved from one grade to the next without specific forethought to what their needs are before, during, and after the move. A grade-level transition represents a multifaceted process that can affect the quality of life of not only the student and family directly involved in the transition, but also the teachers and classmates. While individual activities supporting Julianne's transition from one grade level to the next can be identified from the vignette (e.g., obtaining her class schedule early), transition plans must be more than a compilation of individual activities. Transition planning should include the sending classroom, the interim time between leaving one classroom and entering the next classroom, and the receiving classroom. It is important to observe the student and family after the student has crossed the threshold of the receiving classroom to determine if the transition was successful. Transition activities and events should be, to the fullest extent possible, coordinated via a transition plan that facilitates a positive experience and promotes effective social, academic, and functional outcomes. Finally, transition plans should be based on the individual needs, preferences, and strengths of students and their families (Repetto & Correa, 1996) and incorporate strategies to maximize developmental and programmatic continuity for students and families (Kagan & Neuman, 1998).

## What We Know About Transitions

We must first acknowledge that grade-level transitions may be challenging for any student and his or her family. Indeed, many of the significant grade-level transitions parallel normative developmental shifts (e.g., intellectual, moral, social-emotional, and physical changes) (Bredekamp & Copple, 1997). Such transitions may be particularly challenging for students and families experiencing any type of ongoing developmental or family concerns (e.g., poverty, low parental education, maladaptive family patterns, the presence of a developmental disability, etc.). Developmental and educational transitions can, in and of themselves, disrupt established continuity (or balance). While the presence of non-normative risk can intensify that disruption, effective transition planning can help mediate these effects (Kagan & Neuman, 1998).

Several authors have suggested that students and families find both the anticipation of the transition to a new educational context and their attempts to adjust to new personnel, educational philosophy, curriculum, support, and expectations highly stressful (e.g., Bray, Coleman, & Bracken, 1981; Fewell, 1986; Fowler, Chandler, Johnson, & Stella, 1988; Hains, 1992; Hains, Fowler, & Chandler, 1988; Hanline, 1988; Rule, Fiechtl, & Innocenti, 1990; Sainato & Lyon, 1989; Wolery, 1989). Individual and family stress has been identified as a primary influence on family patterns, which, in turn, directly affect student outcomes (Guralnick, 1997). Thus, we must look beyond basic skill sets (i.e., readiness skills) to the associated contextual variables when considering grade-level transitions (Ramey & Ramey, 1999). For example, in her review of early childhood program research in 13 industrialized and developing countries (Australia, Canada, Colombia, France, Germany, India, Ireland, Japan, Singapore, South Korea, Sweden, Turkey, and the United Kingdom), Spence-Babcock (1995) highlighted the importance of considering not only student skills, but also program quality and family resources and supports. She determined that the quality of the program is increasingly important as family resources and supports decline. Student skills are, of course, related not only to the quality of education and family resources and supports, but also to the developmental characteristics of the student himself. Thus, successful transitions are a function of the transaction of both student skills and contextual supports provided by the family and educational system. A basic model that depicts the primary considerations of grade-level transition planning is presented below.

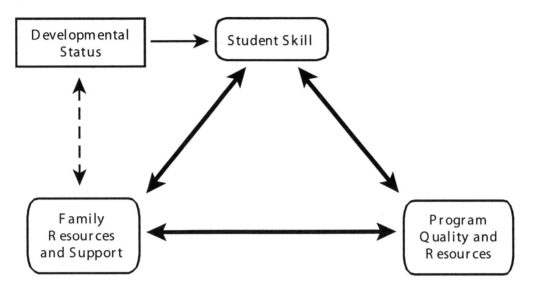

Successful transitions can be facilitated by identification and support of appropriate skills (Hains, 1992; LeAger & Shapiro, 1995; Ramey & Ramey, 1999; Rous & Hallam, 1998; Rule et al., 1990; Sainato & Lyon, 1989); alignment of teacher expectations with actual student skills (LeAger & Shapiro, 1995; Pianta & Cox, 1998; Sainato & Lyon, 1989); description of instructional environments (Early, Pianta, & Cox, 1999; Graue, 1999; Sainato & Lyon, 1989); identification of parent needs and concerns (Christenson, 1999; Hanline, 1988); clear definition of roles for students, family members, and teachers (Fowler et al., 1988; Hains et al., 1988); facilitation of parent involvement (Bredekamp & Copple, 1997; Hartos & Power, 1997; Henderson & Berla, 1994; Horn & West, 1992; Linver & Silverberg, 1997; Paulson, 1994); and promotion of positive teacher attitudes and perceptions (Bender & Ukeje, 1989; Buysse, Wesley, Keyes, & Bailey, 1996; Chow & Winzer, 1992; Diamond, Spiegel-McGill, & Hanrahan, 1988; Hannah & Pliner, 1983; Malouf & Schiller, 1995; Pajares, 1992; Pianta & Cox, 1998). This last variable, teacher attitudes and perceptions, may be particularly important to successful transitions. Teachers who hold negative attitudes toward, are uncomfortable with, or feel less than competent in teaching students with disabilities may develop a bias against these students. This bias may be expressed through misperceptions about students' abilities, lowered expectations for performance, under-crediting of actual performance, or a lack of motivation/initiative to provide optimal instructional opportunities for these students. Such bias is likely to have a strong effect on how, and to what extent, teachers support students' transition into and inclusion in general education classrooms (Hains et al., 1988; Zill, 1999).

To what extent are parents and teachers aware of, and participating in, transition activities? In a study of typical preschool-to-kindergarten transitions conducted through the National Center for Early Development and Learning (Pianta & Cox, 1998), 77 percent of the 3,600 kindergarten teachers surveyed reported that they typically do not receive information about how to facilitate student transition. Furthermore, 75 percent of these teachers had no specialized training related to students' transitions. Teachers identified talking with parents, sending a letter to parents at the beginning of the school year, and holding an open house at the beginning of the school year as the primary strategies for facilitating students' entry into kindergarten. Such activities are the norm for any teacher beginning a new school year and, while useful in a general sense, fall short of meeting the needs of students at risk for, or experiencing, significant developmental or family concerns.

Griebel and Niesel (1997) reported that 90-95 percent of Bavarian kindergarten teachers use an enrollment questionnaire and an enrollment interview as a transition strategy. In addition, parents typically make a preliminary visit to the classroom, accompany their child into the classroom, and stay with their child for a time to help the child adjust to the new environment. Preliminary visits, enrollment questionnaires, and interviews can be useful as planned strategies in providing teachers with unique insights into student and family needs and concerns.

Malone and Troup (2005) reported that kindergarten teachers participating in their preschool-to-kindergarten study were well aware of the supports needed to facilitate the transition of students with disabilities into their general education classrooms (e.g., assistance from specialists, a classroom aide, reduced class size). Unfortunately, nearly half of these teachers indicated that they were not provided adequate transition supports. Nearly all of the teachers were aware of the benefits of their visiting the preschool classroom prior to a student's transition into their kindergarten classroom and, in fact, nearly 75 percent of these teachers were given release time to conduct such visits. Three quarters of these teachers also reported participating in the development of students' IEPs prior to their enrollment in kindergarten. This practice enables sending and receiving teachers to share information and work to promote developmental and programmatic continuity. Two thirds of the Malone and Troup study teachers believed that the type, format, and frequency of communication with parents of students with disabilities was different from communication with other parents. They indicated that individual communications with parents of students with disabilities needed to be more frequent, lengthier, more detailed, varied in format (e.g., daily face-to-face meetings, telephone calls, daily or weekly logs/journals, newsletters, conferences, charts), and open to a greater number of people than communications with parents of students without disabilities (Malone & Troup, in press).

Teachers in the Pianta, Kraft-Sayre, Rimm-Kaufman, Gercke, and Higgins (2001) study typically engaged in the practice of having preschool students visit the kindergarten classroom; Pianta and Cox (1998) reported that 57 percent of kindergarten teachers surveyed held regular meetings with 1st-grade teachers to facilitate effective transitions between programs. Over half of these teachers also have their students visit a 1st-grade class. Unfortunately, over 75 percent of these same teachers reported that they do not attend transition meetings, do not provide parents with information on 1st grade, and do not jointly develop transition plans for students.

Finally, in a statewide survey of parents of students receiving special education services (Academic Information Management, 2004), 55 percent of the parents surveyed did not completely understand the purpose of transition planning. This lack of understanding was a particular problem for parents of intermediate grade students (ages 11-14 years). Only about half of the parents surveyed completely understood that high school to community/work transition planning is critical (and required by U.S. law and some Canadian provincial legislation).

Although progress has been made regarding transition philosophy and practice, the reality of fully appropriate transitions that minimize the discontinuity experienced by students and families as they move through the educational system is not complete (Anderson, Jacobs, Schramm, & Splittgerber, 2000; Shore, 1998). Based on the study results described above, parent and teacher understanding of, and engagement in, transition practices is relatively limited, albeit varied. This reality is underscored in Julianne's experiences with important grade-level transitions. While Julianne was provided certain supports along the way, they were not typically the result of a collaboratively developed plan of action. The cumulative effects of continually failing to formally recognize the importance of, and address the needs associated with, grade-level transitions is borne out clearly in this specific case. A balance must be struck between ideals that *should* exist and the reality that *does* exist. Unfortunately, that which we know should (and could) exist, relative to transition planning, far outweighs that which we are actually doing to promote effective transitions.

## Transition Essentials

The National Association for the Education of Young Children (NAEYC) has identified four elements of successful transitions (Bredekamp & Copple, 1997, p. 122):

1. Ensure program continuity by providing developmentally appropriate curriculum for all age levels in all educational settings
2. Maintain ongoing communication and cooperation between teachers and administrators at different programs
3. Prepare students for the transitions
4. Involve parents in the transitions.

Although these recommendations come from an early childhood (birth through 8 years) organization, they are applicable to all the grade-level transitions discussed in this chapter. To put it bluntly, they just make good sense. School personnel and parents also should note that:

- Transition is a process, not a single action or event
- Transition planning takes time, effort, and understanding on the part of students, parents, and school personnel
- Grade-level transitions bring with them changes in the type of school work required, the quantity of school work required, and expectations regarding the quality of work submitted by students
- Students are increasingly challenged across all areas of development as they advance in grade
- Effective transition planning requires collaboration and communication among stakeholders (students, parents, and school personnel) regarding such issues as student characteristics, curriculum, program organization, student and parent needs and concerns, and teacher expectations
- Students with disabilities are not likely to automatically conform to program expectations; hence, the transition process must be carefully planned, executed, and evaluated
- Students can and should become increasingly involved in the development of their own transition plans as they move through the grades.

## Transition Plans Support Basic Human Needs

The specifics of any transition plan are dependent upon the individual needs, preferences, and strengths of students and their families. As noted by Glasser (1985), all people have a need for balance in their lives and, thus, strive for a good fit between the real world and the world they would ideally have. Everyone's ability to achieve balance is mediated by the extent to which they can meet five basic, genetically instructed, human needs: survival, belonging, competence, pleasure, and choice. The attempts by many students with disabilities and their families to realize even the most basic of these human needs become compromised by the challenges set before them in educational contexts. If we make survival (safety) a given for most students (though this is not always the case), we must then ask ourselves the following questions:

- To what extent do students with disabilities and their families feel as though they belong? Do they feel as though they are a meaningful part of the school?
- To what extent do students with disabilities and their families feel as though they are competent? Are they able to be successful in the classroom and to successfully navigate the social and administrative context of the general and special education system?
- To what extent do students with disabilities and their families find their school experiences pleasurable? Is school and its related events (carnivals, IEP meetings, concerts) something that they actually look forward to attending?
- To what extent do students with disabilities and their families feel as though they have real choices related to educational opportunities? Are real options and opportunities to choose "on the table," or do school personnel present only select alternatives cleverly disguised as options?

Effective grade-level transition plans build community and are responsive to specific student and family needs, concerns, and developmental status through the provision of appropriate multi-faceted supports (Bohan-Baker & Little, 2002; Kraft-Sayre & Pianta, 2000; Schumacher, 1998). Such plans enable the student, parents, and school personnel to identify adaptive anchor points for the student's cognitive and social-emotional maps that not only establish meaning for the student, but also, in so doing, help promote continuity (Koizumi, 2000). While not a cure-all, effective transition planning can address many challenges either before they materialize or, at the very least, in a timely fashion.

## Significant Transition Points

As stated earlier, transitions can be considered grade-to-grade or at critical junctures, marked by relatively substantive, qualitative changes across grade levels. Specific receiving-grade factors may help us understand and plan for associated transitions. The individualized nature of how students and families experience and respond to significant transitions is critical, as is the fact that the number of transition activities provided is related to a variety of positive outcomes including positive adjustment, increased achievement, and lowered drop-out rates (Hartos & Power, 1997; Henderson & Berla, 1994; Hertzog & Morgan, 1999; Horn & West, 1992; Linver & Silverberg, 1997; MacIver, 1990; MacIver & Epstein, 1991; Margetts, 1999; Paulson, 1994; Ramey & Ramey, 1999).

## Preschool-to-Kindergarten Considerations

The preschool-to-kindergarten transition has been considered by many as the most significant transition in the lives of students and families (Bohan-Baker & Little, 2002; Meisels, 1999; Pianta et al., 2001). This transition is typically marked by the student's physical relocation to a new school building, a qualitative shift in program structure and curricular philosophies, and a revision of one's self-perception (identity). For example, kindergarten programs typically include less play, less choice, and more teacher direction than preschool programs (Peters, 2000; Troup & Malone 2002). Changes such as these, in addition to the loss of a dense student/family/school support network, can induce stress and anxiety among both students and families, which can negatively influence both cognitive and social competence (Griebel & Niesel, 1997, 1999; O'Brien, 1991; Ramey & Ramey, 1999; Shore, 1998). Data reported by both Pianta and Cox (1998) and Griebel and Niesel (1997) indicate that nearly half of all kindergarten students experience transition problems. The transition of students with disabilities into general education kindergarten also can be stressful to teachers, many of whom report a need for additional classroom supports as well as more communication with parents of students with disabilities (Malone & Troup, 2005). Thus, students, families, and teachers experience challenges during this particular grade-level transition.

Teachers' reports of readiness skills vary considerably. Furthermore, a wide range of skill indicators is provided in various assessment instruments (e.g., Battelle Developmental Inventory, Transdisciplinary Play-Based Assessment, Carolina Curriculum, etc.). Thus, any presentation of a basic skill set must be viewed with this variety in mind. With this caution noted, the skills reported by teachers as essential for kindergarten success include following directions; demonstrating self-help skills (e.g., toileting, communication of needs, safety); socially engaging others; sharing; recognizing letters, numbers, and shapes; counting to 10; understanding 1-to-1 correspondence between spoken numbers and objects; understanding concepts of "more," "less," and "equal"; sitting and attending in group activities; working independently and cooperatively; understanding concepts of "same" and "different"; and having basic gross and fine motor skills (e.g., walking, hopping, holding a crayon) (Griebel & Niesel, 1997, 1999; Malone & Troup, 2005; Nurse, 1987; Pianta & Cox, 1998, Troup & Malone, 2002; Zill & West, 2001). A student's demonstration of requisite skills is related to other variables, such as age of the student at kindergarten entry (older students are likely to be more competent); family risk factors (certain family risks, including poverty, low parent education, and maladaptive family patterns, negatively influence student competence); developmental status (students with disabilities are less likely to demonstrate basic skills than are same-age peers); instructional strategies (structured, teacher-directed teaching supports children's basic skill acquisition, but hinders the acquisition of basic social skills); and supports provided (parent and teacher supports can mediate negative influences) (Bohan-Baker & Little, 2002; Hartos & Power, 1997; Henderson & Berla, 1994; Horn & West, 1992; Linver & Silverberg, 1997; Paulson, 1994; Pianta & Cox, 1998; Pianta et al., 2001; Stipek, 2004; Stipek et al., 1998; Tudge, Odero, Hogan, & Etz, 2003; Zill & West, 2001).

In Julianne's case, a formal transition plan might have outlined her educational needs prior to the beginning of the school year rather than three weeks into the year, when she and the other students are becoming adjusted to the program and people. Such a plan might have focused on Julianne receiving full-day kindergarten in the general education classroom, with appropriate supports and accommodations. At the very least, the plan would have ensured the participation of all stakeholders in the process, rather than the introduction of a new team member (special education teacher) and a new schedule several weeks into the school year.

## Kindergarten-to-Primary Considerations

Of each of the grade-level transitions discussed in this chapter, the kindergarten-to-primary grade (e.g., 1st grade) transition has possibly received the least attention. However, this particular transition may be important for helping students establish a sound base for their time in the primary grades and beyond (Entwisle & Alexander, 1999). What skills are expected for the 1st grade? Ideally, students develop increased independence, revise their social roles and network (e.g., fitting in becomes increasingly important), strive for increased independence and ownership of their own learning, and are expected to become more responsible and make appropriate choices. Furthermore, the curriculum typically becomes more traditional (i.e., academically focused and teacher-directed), homework is introduced, the school day moves from half-day to full-day, and grades become increasingly emphasized. Students are expected to learn to use reading strategies and develop comprehension skills, demonstrate basic writing skills, count and write numerals to 100, and develop basic addition and subtraction skills (Entwisle & Alexander, 1999; Griebel & Niesel, 1999; Gurian, Goodman, & Schwartz, 2005; Pianta & Cox, 1998; American School Counselor Association, 2005).

Broström (2000) suggested that one of the most significant barriers to kindergarten-to-primary grade transition is the bridging of educational philosophies. The move to 1st grade requires an adjustment from a more student-oriented and play-based program structure to a more teacher-directed and academically focused curriculum (Henry, Gordon, Henderson, & Ponder, 2003). Given the purpose of transition planning to promote feelings of well-being and belonging, "the teacher and the environment she creates must take the child's perceptions, interests and needs into account" (Broström, 2000, p. 2). While communication among stakeholders is critical (Brostrom, 2000; Fabian, 2000; Griebel & Niesel, 1999), we also must consider reports that most elementary teachers typically have little training related to working with parents; consequently, we tend to see a decline in parent involvement as students progress through the grade levels (Bohan-Baker & Little, 2002; Entwisle, 1995; Epstein, Coates, Salines, Sanders, & Simon, 1997).

## Primary/Junior-to-Intermediate Grade Considerations

The primary/junior grade-to-intermediate grade (e.g., 6th or 7th grade) transition represents, in most cases, yet another programmatic shift combined with a physical relocation. Students must orient themselves to a new school "map" (e.g., finding lockers, class changes), new curriculum (e.g., format, content, expectations), new social structure (e.g., a shift in social context), and new social expectations (e.g., peer influence and increased interest in boyfriends/girlfriends). They also experience new intellectual challenges as the academic work becomes more rigorous, as well as new physical challenges with the imminent onset of puberty. Subject matter becomes significantly more detailed as teachers become specialists in specific areas of study (literature, math, science, history, etc.). At this age, students are becoming more aware of themselves and others as individuals. They are expected to communicate relatively effectively, work cooperatively with minimum supervision, coordinate a schedule of unrelated courses/assignments, demonstrate self-control, and resolve conflicts peacefully (Anderson et al., 2000; Elias, 1993; Feldlaufer, Midgley, & Eccles, 1988; Gurian et al., 2005; Mitman & Packer, 1982;

Rice, 1997; Richardson, 2005; Rubin-Berger, 2004; Schulenberg, Asp, & Peterson, 1984; Schumacher, 1998; Wigfield & Eccles, 1994). The increased focus on testing is a particular concern for students with disabilities.

Given the multiple significant academic, social, and physical changes that students experience during this grade-level transition, it is not a complete surprise that many students develop poor perceptions of their own competence, experience psychological distress and lowered self-esteem, and exhibit declines in achievement (Anderman & Midgley, 1997; Chung, Elias, & Schneider, 1998; Schulenberg et al., 1984; Wigfield & Eccles, 1994; Wigfield, Eccles, MacIver, Reuman, & Midgley, 1991). The decrease in student-centered decision-making and whole-class (versus cooperative group) work, and the increase in teacher directiveness associated with intermediate school curricula may contribute to these negative trends (Feldlaufer et al., 1988; Midgley & Feldlaufer, 1987; Ward, Mergendoller, & Tikunoff, 1982). Feldlaufer et al. (1988) also report that "post-transition teachers are characterized as less caring, warm, friendly, and supportive than pre-transition teachers" (p. 151). The apparent lack of fit between students and classroom context may make it extremely challenging for students to establish the adaptive anchor points needed for deriving meaning from, and meeting, basic human needs (i.e., survival, competence, belonging, pleasure, and choice) in the intermediate grade environment (Feldlaufer et al., 1988; Glasser, 1985; Koizumi, 2000). The good news is that not all students are significantly affected by these factors, and many of those who are will rebound. The bad news is, for students who experience cultural, familial, and/or developmental risk or disability, these factors can create crisis and eventual maladaptation (McCubbin & Patterson, 1981).

**Intermediate-to-Secondary Considerations**
As was the case with the primary/junior-to-intermediate grade transition discussed above, the intermediate-to-secondary (e.g., 9th grade) transition is marked by both a programmatic shift and a physical relocation. Students must once again experience a change in their known social structure/expectations and orient themselves to a new school "map," new curriculum format, content, and expectations. For example, school size, diversity of student population, and the number of students increases dramatically over that experienced in intermediate school. Friendship networks can evolve as students meet new people and move away from old friends. These changes can produce anxiety and stress within students. Other social issues include the intensification of peer influence and the pressure to fit in; increased importance of dating; the emergence of pressures to experiment with sex, alcohol, and drugs; and feelings of cognitive and emotional dissonance between becoming more independent from parents and needing/wanting parent supports. Academic rigor intensifies and students are expected to be internally motivated and independent learners. They are expected to demonstrate effective study skills, be self-controlled, have effective organizational skills, and become increasingly responsible for their decisions. Students, parents, and teachers begin to make decisions about university preparation or vocational programs of study. Finally, assessment of competency becomes more high stakes, students are expected to begin planning how they will meet credit requirements for graduation, and an emphasis emerges on entering the adult world (Campbell, 2001; Gurian et al., 2005; Hertzog & Morgan, 1998; Letrello & Miles, 2003; Litner, 2003; Mizelle, 1999; Mizelle & Irvin, 2005; Morgan & Hertzog, 2001; Zeedyk et al., 2003).

The collateral and transactional nature of developmental, academic, and social transitions results in an increasingly complex set of circumstances with increasingly higher stakes for students, parents, and teachers. At each critical transition point, students who experience cultural, familial, or developmental concerns are at increased risk for further differentiation from their peer group. The challenges associated with the intermediate-to-secondary transition, while not so very different from earlier transitions on the surface (i.e., each transition carries with it greater expectations for academic performance), may be qualitatively different with respect to the importance attributed to them by students, parents, and teachers. Students experiencing cultural, familial, or developmental difficulties may lack sufficient resources to cope with transition-related challenges. In addition, students experiencing a constellation of concerns (as many students with disabilities do) may find themselves in extreme jeopardy. For example, data from the National Longitudinal Transition Study of Special Education Students (Wagner & Blackorby, 1996) and from the National Council on Disability (2000) report on transition and post-school outcomes for youth with disabilities show that 30 percent of students with disabilities in the United States do not graduate from high school. The academic expectations and social milieu require skills that many children (e.g., those experiencing ADHD) simply do not have (Litner, 2003). In short, transition planning is not discretionary; it is a necessity that may serve as a veritable lifeline for many students.

## Postsecondary Considerations

Up to this point, each transition has had a school program as the receiving environment. Such is not the primary case when we consider postsecondary transitions for students with disabilities. Indeed, the postsecondary transition is focused on the student's preparation to enter "the adult world." The attention of students and parents is often directed to issues of self-identity, self-advocacy, independent living, personal responsibility, securing employment, and postsecondary education. Transition planning team members should include the student, family members, school administrator, special education teacher, vocational education teacher, general education teacher (if the student has been enrolled in general education classes), school psychologist, school counselors (guidance and vocational rehabilitation), social worker, community agency provider(s), and any other person or professional who is relevant to the student's life (e.g., developmental therapist, recreation and leisure therapist, friends). Preparatory activities often include working with a job coach, investigating community resources and supports (e.g., service agencies, bus routes, employment options, housing/residential options, postsecondary education opportunities), critically evaluating functional skills, exploring financial aid and estate planning options, and investigating leisure options (deFur, 2002; Merchant & Gajar, 1997; Timmons, McIntyre, Whitney-Thomas, Butterworth, & Allen, 1998; White, Edelman, & Schuyler, 2001).

The postsecondary transition marks the end of the primary system of service delivery that students and parents have known for nearly two decades (Timmons et al., 1998), and so it is a stressful process for students and parents alike. Indeed, students with disabilities are at extreme risk for school failure, with only a 70 percent chance of graduation (National Council on Disability, 2000; Wagner & Blackorby, 1996). Those students who do graduate have the most adaptive internal and external resources and supports. However, even these students do not realize the level of postsecondary success that we would expect, given their resources and supports (National Council on Disability, 2000; Wagner & Blackorby, 1996; Wood & Cronnin, 1999). Indeed, these "successful" students typically experience low rates of employment, low rates of postsecondary education, and increased reliance on public assistance. It is clear that transition planning is essential to the quality of life of students with disabilities and their families.

Reflecting on Julianne's pre-graduation experiences, we are left with many questions. Why did Julianne not have a high school plan for working toward a diploma? How is it that Julianne and her parents were not aware that she would not be receiving a diploma until it was too late to address their concerns? Why didn't Julianne have a formal transition plan? The answer to these questions might lie, in part, in the data on actual service provision. In the United States, where federal law requires the development and implementation of postsecondary transition plans, 76 percent of the states are noncompliant regarding team member requirements, 70 percent of the states are noncompliant regarding notification requirements, and 68 percent of the states are noncompliant regarding statements of needed services (National Council on Disability, 2000). If federal law cannot ensure the provision of services, then how can they be ensured? In short, no student who needs support that can be provided through a reasonable planning process should be allowed to simply pass through the educational system, especially during the final years that serve as a springboard into adulthood.

## Recommendations

In an ideal world, each critical transition point in the educational life of students with disabilities would be grounded in a collaboratively developed, effective transition plan. Each plan would outline the resources and supports needed to maximize the student's chance of success and, across each critical transition point, would have a positive and cumulative effect on the life of the student. Unfortunately, life is rarely ideal, and truly effective transition planning on any large scale eludes us.

In a thorough analysis of the historic-social-political context of educational transition (reform) in Central-Eastern European countries, Rado (2001) outlines five points of leverage for effective policy-making: 1) improved educational management, 2) educational accountability via assessment and evaluation, 3) quality assurance within the systemic environment of schools, 4) stakeholder involvement and public discourse, and 5) capacity building. Interestingly, these same concepts can be readily applied to our topic of grade-level transitions and, in so doing, facilitate a fundamental change in the availability of, and access to, transition-oriented supports by students with disabilities and their families. With this being said, we acknowledge the work that has been done to promote transition

---

**Significant Transitions**

Preschool to Kindergarten
Kindergarten to Primary
Primary to Junior/Intermediate
Intermediate to Secondary
Secondary to Postsecondary
Secondary to Work

*each transition has its own considerations

---

planning by offering the following recommendations based on this work:

- Provide high-quality education to all stakeholders (students, parents, school personnel) about the purpose of, need for, and strategies supporting transition planning.
- Carefully and critically examine current policies and practices related to transition planning. If the current policies and practices are not appropriate—if they do not consistently result in positive outcomes for students—then work to change the policies and/or practices.
- Formally evaluate the school environment with the intent of identifying facilitating or adaptive resources and stressors related to policies, people, perceptions, practices, places, and props. While many variables exist that we cannot anticipate, we are often surprised, when we take the time to look carefully, at how many resources and stressors are a standard part of our school environment.
- Provide teachers with adequate and appropriate supports (e.g., funding) so that they can reasonably engage in the practice of transition planning and implementation.
- Make every possible effort to ensure that meaningful transition plans are being developed, that this process is team-based and collaborative, and that parents and other relevant family members are meaningful and contributing team members.
- Use frequent, and multiple modes of, communication to reach as many students and parents as possible.
- Develop articulation agreements between programs at critical transition points so that teachers at both ends of the transition bridge understand each other's program content and expectations.
- Prepare a summary of student strengths and challenges related to learning and behavior as a tool for discourse, reflection, and planning.
- Make program visits to develop a better understanding of the sending and receiving programs. Students, parents, and teachers should all make program visits. Visits will minimally include communication among stakeholders, but also may include formal orientation to new schools and programs, visitation to classes in progress, shadowing (e.g., the incoming student accompanies the older student), etc.
- Strive to be aware of the power of perceptions. Is the "problem" truly inherent in the student, or is it in how the teacher perceives the student and family?
- Be aware of how good the fit is between the skills of the student and their expectations for that student. Efforts should be made to improve the match if it is not already appropriate. This does not always mean that the student has to make the accommodations.
- Change the current practice of assigning students to a classroom just prior to the start of school so that teachers have time to collaboratively develop transition plans.
- Be creative and collaborative in identifying activities that can support the transition process (e.g., putting on social events for students, parents, and teachers; establishing a pen-pal program that connects incoming students with older students; implementing a mentor program along the lines of the Big Brother/Big Sister program and Parent-to-Parent whereby new students/parents are paired with experienced students/parents; creating Internet sites that students and parents can visit, etc.).

*(These recommendations are based on: Bohan-Baker & Little, 2002; Bredekamp & Copple, 1997; Campbell, 2001; Gurian et al., 2005; Hertzog & Morgan, 1998, 1999; Letrello & Miles, 2003; Mizelle, 1999; Pantleo, 1999; Rubin-Berger, 2004; Schumacher, 1998; Timmons et al., 1998).*

## Sample of Resources Available

Many outstanding resources on transition planning are available in print, electronic, video, and audio formats. For example, typing *"Transition Planning"* + *"Disability"* into an Internet search yielded over 24,000 hits, and included global, national, state, local, and individual resources. Seven specific sites that included useful information and resources are:

- National Dissemination Center for Children With Disabilities (NICHCY)
  www.nichcy.org/pubs/transum/ts10txt.htm
  *Transition Planning: A Team Effort* (deFur, 2002) includes valuable information on the process of transition planning, case examples of the process, a list of organizations with Internet links, and a publications list.
- Transition Research Institute (at Illinois)
  www.ed.uiuc.edu/sped/tri/transitionresources.html
  The site provides a publications list, curriculum and planning guides, a list of videos, and transcripts from transition audio conferences.
- National Center on Secondary Education and Transition
  http://ncset.jaws.umn.edu/default.asp
  Site includes a publications list, Internet sites, and an events calendar.
- Family and Child Transitions Into Least Restrictive Environments (FACTS/LRE) Information Series
  http://facts.crc.uiuc.edu
  Site includes links to the five publications developed for the series: *Interagency Agreements, Entering a New Preschool, Facilitating Inclusion in Community Settings, Planning Your Child's Transition to Preschool*, and *Writing an Interagency Agreement on Transition*. It also includes an information sheet on an extended school year and links to other Internet sites. Each publication in the series includes valuable information on its designated topic and handouts that can be used for training/dissemination.
- Transition Coalition
  www.transitioncoalition.org/bestpractices/index.shtml
  Site includes a three-session, self-paced "course" on best practices in transition planning.
- Family Voices
  www.familyvillage.wisc.edu/sp/TRANS.HTML
  *Family Voices & the Internet* is an extensive inventory of transition resources available via the Internet. Resources are organized into many categories, including: General Information, Career Interest Inventories, Independent Living, Employment, Health, Civil Rights and Legal Information, Post-Secondary Education, Transportation, Programs and Benefits, and Supports for Youth and Young Adults.
- *Dare To Dream (Revised): A Guide To Plan Your Future*
  www.firn.edu/doe/commhome/pdf/dream.pdf
  The link produces a Portable Document Format (PDF) of the *Dare To Dream* guide developed for students to assist them in planning for their futures. The guide also can help parents and professionals understand the transition process.

# References

Academic Information Management. (2004). *Statewide survey of parents of students receiving special education services*. Austin, TX: Author.

*American Heritage Dictionary* (4th ed.). (2002). Boston: Houghton Mifflin.

American School Counselor Association. (2005). *First grade basic skills*. Retrieved February 23, 2005, from www.teachervision.fen.com/teaching-methods/curriculum_planning/2843.html?detoured:1

Anderman, E. M., & Midgley, C. (1997). Changes in achievement goal orientations, perceived academic competence, and grades across the transition to middle-level schools. *Contemporary Educational Psychology, 22*, 269–298.

Anderson, L. W., Jacobs, J., Schramm, S., & Splittgerber, F. (2000). School transitions: Beginning of the end or a new beginning? *International Journal of Educational Research, 33*, 325-339.

Bender, W. N., & Ukeje, I. C. (1989). Instructional strategies in mainstream classrooms: Prediction of the strategies teachers select. *Remedial and Special Education, 10*, 23-30.

Bohan-Baker, M., & Little, P. M. D. (2002). *The transition to kindergarten: A review of current research and promising practices to involve families*. Harvard Family Research Project.

Bray, N., Coleman, J., & Bracken, M. (1981). Critical events in parenting handicapped children. *Journal of Division of Early Childhood, 3*(1), 26-33.

Bredekamp, S., & Copple, C. (Eds.). (1997). *Developmentally appropriate practice in early childhood programs* (rev. ed.). Washington, DC: National Association for the Education of Young Children.

Broström, S. (2000, September). *Communication and continuity in the transition from kindergarten to school in Denmark*. Paper presented at the 10th European Conference on the Quality of Early Childhood Education, London, England. Retrieved March 9, 2005, from http://extranet.edfac.unimelb.edu.au/LED/tec/pdf/brostrom.pdf.

Buysse, V., Wesley, P., Keyes, L., & Bailey, D. B. (1996). Assessing the comfort zone of child care teachers serving young children with disabilities. *Journal of Early Intervention, 29*(3), 189-203.

Campbell, H. (2001). Easing the transition to high school. *The Education Digest, 67*(1), 12-18.

Chow, P., & Winzer, M. M. (1992). Reliability and validity of a scale measuring attitudes toward mainstreaming. *Education and Psychological Measurement, 52*, 223-228.

Christenson, S. L. (1999). Families and schools: Rights, responsibilities, resources, and relationships. In R. C. Pianta & M. J. Cox (Eds.), *The transition to kindergarten* (pp. 143-177). Baltimore: Paul H. Brookes.

Chung, H., Elias, M., & Schneider, K. (1998). Patterns of individual adjustment changes during middle school transition. *Journal of School Psychology, 36*(1), 83-101.

deFur, S. (2002). *Transition planning: A team effort*. National Dissemination Center for Children with Disabilities (TS10). Retrieved January 29, 2005, from www.nichcy.org.

Diamond, K. E., Spiegel-McGill, P., & Hanrahan, P. (1988). Planning for school transition: An ecological developmental approach. *Journal of the Division for Early Childhood, 12*, 245-252.

Early, D., Pianta, R., & Cox, M. (1999). Kindergarten teachers and classrooms: A transition context. *Early Education and Development, 10*(1), 24-46.

Elias, M. J. (1993). *Social decision making and life skills development guidelines for middle school educators*. Gaithersburg, MD: Aspen.

Entwisle, D. R. (1995). The role of schools in sustaining benefits of early childhood programs. *The Future of Children, 5*(3), 133-144.

Entwisle, D. R., & Alexander, K. L. (1999). Early schooling and social stratification. In R. C. Pianta & M. Cox (Eds.), *The transition to kindergarten: Research, policy, training, and practice* (pp. 13-38). Baltimore: Paul H. Brookes.

Epstein, J. L., Coates, L., Salines, K. C., Sanders, M. G., & Simon, B. S. (1997). *School, family, and community partnerships: Your handbook for action.* Thousand Oaks, CA: Corwin Press.

Fabian, H. (2000, September). *A seamless transition?* Paper presented at the 10th European Conference on the Quality of Early Childhood Education, London, England. Retrieved March 9, 2005, from http://extranet.edfac.unimelb.edu.au/LED/tec/pdf/fabian1.pdf.

Feldlaufer, H., Midgley, C., & Eccles, J. S. (1988). Student, teacher, and observer perceptions of the classroom environment before and after the transition to junior high school. *Journal of Early Adolescence, 8*, 133–156.

Fewell, R. R. (1986). A handicapped child in the family. In R. R. Fewell & P. F. Vadasy (Eds.), *Families of handicapped children* (pp. 3-34). Austin, TX: Pro-Ed.

Fowler, S. A., Chandler, L. K., Johnson, T. E., & Stella, M. E. (1988). Individualizing family involvement in school transitions: Gathering information and choosing the next program. *Journal of the Division for Early Childhood, 12*(3), 208-216.

Glasser, W. (1985). *Control theory: A new explanation of how we control our lives.* New York: Harper & Row.

Graue, E. (1999). Diverse perspectives on kindergarten contexts and practices. In R.C. Pianta & M. J. Cox (Eds), *The transition to kindergarten* (pp. 109-142). Baltimore: Paul H. Brookes.

Griebel, W., & Niesel, R. (1997, September). *From family to kindergarten: A common experience in a transition perspective.* Paper presented at the 7th European Conference on the Quality of Early Childhood Education, Munich, Germany. Retrieved March 9, 2005, from http://extranet.edfac.unimelb.edu.au/LED/tec/pdf/griebelniesel3.pdf.

Griebel, W., & Niesel, R. (1999, September). *From kindergarten to school: A transition for the family.* Paper presented at the 9th European Conference on the Quality of Early Childhood Education, Helsinki, Finland. Retrieved March 9, 2005, from http://extranet.edfac.unimelb.edu.au/LED/tec/pdf/griebel-niesel2.pdf.

Guralnick, M. J. (Ed.). (1997). *The effectiveness of early intervention.* Baltimore: Paul H. Brookes.

Gurian, A., Goodman, R. F., & Schwartz, S. (2005). *Transition points: Helping students start, change, and move through the grades.* Retrieved February 5, 2005, from www.aboutourkids.org.

Hains, A. H. (1992). Strategies for preparing preschool children with special needs for the kindergarten mainstream. *Journal of Early Intervention, 16*(4), 320-333.

Hains, A. H., Fowler, S. A., & Chandler, L. K. (1988). Planning school transitions: Family and professional collaboration. *Journal of the Division for Early Childhood, 12*(2), 108-115.

Hanline, M. F. (1988). Making the transition to preschool: Identification of parent needs. *Journal of the Division for Early Childhood, 12*(2), 98-107.

Hannah, M. E., & Pliner, S. (1983). Teacher attitudes toward handicapped children: A review and synthesis. *School Psychology Review, 12*(1), 12-25.

Hartos, J. L., & Power, T. G. (1997). Mothers' awareness of their early adolescents' stressors: Relation between awareness and adolescent adjustment. *Journal of Early Adolescence, 17*(4), 371-389.

Henderson, A., & Berla, N. (1994). *A new generation of evidence: The family is critical to student achievement.* Columbia, MD: National Committee for Citizens in Education.

Henry, G. T., Gordon, C. S., Henderson, L. W., & Ponder, B. D. (2003). *Georgia pre-k longitudinal study: Final report, 1996-2001.* Atlanta, GA: Education Policy Group, Andrew Young School of Policy Studies.

Hertzog, C. J., & Morgan, P. L. (1998). Breaking the barriers between middle school and high school:

Developing a transition team for student success. *National Association of Secondary School Principals Bulletin, 82*(5), 94-98.

Hertzog, C. J., & Morgan, P. L. (1999). Making the transition from middle level to high school. *High School Magazine, 6*(4), 26-30.

Horn, L., & West, J. (1992). *National education longitudinal study of 1988: A profile of parents of eighth graders.* Washington, DC: U.S. Government Printing Office.

*Individuals With Disabilities Education Improvements Act.* (2004). 20 USC § 1400 et seq.

Kagan, S. L., & Neuman, M. J. (1998). Lessons from three decades of transition research. *The Elementary School Journal, 98*(4), 365-379.

Koizumi, R. (2000). Anchor points in transitions to a new school environment. *The Journal of Primary Prevention, 20*(3), 175-187.

Kraft-Sayre, M. E., & Pianta, R. C. (2000). *Enhancing the transition to kindergarten: Linking children, families, and schools.* Charlottesville, VA: University of Virginia, National Center for Early Development & Learning.

LeAger, C., & Shapiro, E. (1995). Template matching as a strategy for assessment of and intervention for preschool students with disabilities. *Topics in Early Childhood Special Education, 15*(2), 187-218.

Letrello, T. M., & Miles, D. D. (2003). The transition from middle school to high school: Students with and without learning disabilities share their perceptions. *Clearing House, 76*(4), 212-218.

Linver, M. R., & Silverberg, S. B. (1997). Maternal predictors of early adolescent achievement-related outcomes: Adolescent gender as moderator. *Journal of Early Adolescence, 17*(3), 294-318.

Litner, B. (2003). Teens with ADHD: The challenge of high school. *Child & Youth Care Forum, 32*(3), 137-158.

MacIver, D. J. (1990). Meeting the needs of young adolescents: Advisory groups, interdisciplinary teaching teams, and school transition programs. *Phi Delta Kappan, 71*(6), 458-464.

MacIver, D. J., & Epstein, J. L. (1991). Responsive practices in the middle grades: Teacher teams, advisory groups, remedial instruction, and school transition programs. *American Journal of Education, 99*(4), 587-622.

Malone, D. M., & Troup, K. S. (2005). Contextual factors supporting the transition of preschool children with disabilities into general education kindergarten. *Journal of Early Education and Family Review, 13*(1), 3-18.

Malone, D. M., & Troup, K. S. (in press). Kindergarten teachers' perceptions about the transition of preschool children with disabilities into general education classrooms. *Early Childhood Education Journal.*

Malouf, D. B., & Schiller, E. P. (1995). Practice and research in special education. *Exceptional Children, 61*, 414-421.

Margetts, K. (1999, July). *Transition to school: Looking forward.* Paper presented at the AECA National Conference, Darwin, Australia. Retrieved February 19, 2005, from http://extranet.edfac.unimelb.edu.au/LED/tec/pdf/margetts1.pdf.

McCubbin, H. I., & Patterson, J. M. (1981, October). *Family stress and adaptation to crises: A double ABCX model of family behavior.* Paper presented at the Annual Meeting of the National Council on Family Relations, Milwaukee, WI.

Meisels, S. J. (1999). Assessing readiness. In R. C. Pianta & M. Cox (Eds.), *The transition to kindergarten: Research, policy, training, and practice* (pp. 39-66). Baltimore: Paul H. Brookes.

Merchant, D. J., & Gajar, A. (1997). A review of the literature on self advocacy components in transition programs for students with learning disabilities. *Journal of Vocational Rehabilitation, 8*(3), 223-231.

*Merriam & Webster online dictionary.* Retrieved January 23, 2005, from www.m-w.com/diction-ary/transition.

Midgley, C., & Feldlaufer, H. (1987). Students' and teachers' decision-making fit before and after the transition to junior high school. *Journal of Early Adolescence, 7,* 225-241.

Mitman, A. L., & Packer, M. J. (1982). Concerns of seventh-graders about their transition to junior high school. *Journal of Early Adolescence, 2*(4), 319-338.

Mizelle, N. B. (1999). *Helping middle school students make the transition into high school.* (ERIC Digest). Champaign, IL: ERIC Clearinghouse on Elementary and Early Childhood Education. (ERIC Document Reproduction Service No. ED432411)

Mizelle, N. B., & Irvin, J. L. (2005). *Transition from middle school into high school.* Westerville, OH: National Middle School Association.

Morgan, L. P., & Hertzog, C. J. (2001). Designing comprehensive transitions. *Principal Leadership, 1*(7), 10-18.

National Council on Disability. (2000). *Transition and post-school outcomes for youth with disabilities: Closing the gaps to post-secondary education and employment.* Washington, DC: Author.

Nurse, J. R. (1987). *Readiness for kindergarten.* Retrieved February 12, 2005, from www.kidsource.com/kidsource/content3/READINESS_FOR_K.html

O'Brien, M. (1991). *Promoting successful transitions into school: A review of current intervention practices.* Lawrence, KS: The University of Kansas Early Childhood Research Institute.

Pajares, M. F. (1992). Teachers' beliefs and educational research: Cleaning up a messy construct. *Review of Educational Research, 62,* 307-332.

Pantleo, S. (1999). Making connections to ease the transition from eighth to ninth grade. *High School Magazine, 6*(4), 31.

Paulson, S. E. (1994). Relations of parenting style and parental involvement with ninth-grade students' achievement. *Journal of Early Adolescence, 14*(2), 250-267.

Peters, S. (2000, September). *Multiple perspectives on continuity in early learning and the transition to school.* Paper presented at the 10th European Conference on the Quality of Early Childhood Education, London, England. Retrieved March 9, 2005, from http://extranet.edfac.unimelb.edu.au/LED/tec/pdf/peters1.pdf.

Pianta, R. C., & Cox, M. (1998). *Kindergarten transition.* NCEDL Spotlights Series No. 1. Chapel Hill, NC: National Center for Early Development and Learning.

Pianta, R. C., Kraft-Sayre, M., Rimm-Kaufman, S., Gercke, N., & Higgins, T. (2001). Collaboration in building partnerships between families and schools: The National Center for Early Development and Learning's kindergarten transition intervention. *Early Childhood Research Quarterly, 16,* 117–132.

Pianta, R. C., Rimm-Kaufmann, S. E., & Cox, M. J. (1999). Introduction: An ecological approach to kindergarten transition. In R. C. Pianta & M. J. Cox (Eds.), *The transtion to kindergarten* (pp. 3-12). Baltimore: Paul H. Brookes.

Rado, P. (2001). *Transition in education: Policy making and the key educational policy areas in the Central-European and Baltic countries.* Budapest, Hungary: Open Society Institute for Educational Policy. Retrieved March 13, 2005, from www.osi.hu/iep.

Ramey, C. T., & Ramey, S. L. (1999). Beginning school for children at risk. In R. C. Pianta & M. Cox (Eds.), *The transition to kindergarten: Research, policy, training, and practice* (pp. 217-252). Baltimore: Paul H. Brookes.

Repetto, J. B., & Correa, V. I. (1996). Expanding views on transition. *Exceptional Children, 62*(6), 551-563.

Rice, J. K. (1997). *Explaining the negative impact of the transition from middle to high school on student performance in mathematics and science: An examination of school discontinuity and student background variables.* Paper presented at the Annual Meeting of the American Educational Research Association, Chicago, IL.

Richardson, T. L. (2005). *The importance of emotional intelligence during transition into middle school.* Westerville, OH: National Middle School Association.

Rous, B., & Hallam, R. A. (1998). Easing the transition to kindergarten: Assessment of social, behavioral, and functional skills in young children with disabilities. *Young Exceptional Children, 1*(4), 17-26.

Rubin-Berger, D. (2004). *Easing the middle school transition.* Retrieved December 3, 2004, from http://familyeducation.com/article/0%2C1120%2C3-15234%2C00.html?yf_home.

Rule, S., Fiechtl, B. J., & Innocenti, M. S. (1990). Preparation for transition to mainstreamed post-preschool environments: Development of a survival skills curriculum. *Topics in Early Childhood Special Education, 9,* 78-90.

Sainato, D. M., & Lyon, S. R. (1989). Promoting successful mainstreaming transitions for handicapped preschool children. *Journal of Early Intervention, 13*(4), 305-314.

Schulenberg, J. E., Asp, C. E., & Peterson, A. E. (1984). School from the young adolescnt's perspective: A descriptive report. *Journal of Early Adolescence, 4*(2), 107-130.

Schumacher, D. (1998). *The transition to middle school.* (ERIC Digest). Champaign, IL: ERIC Clearinghouse on Elementary and Early Childhood Education. (ERIC Document Reproduction Service No. ED422119)

Shore, R. (1998). *Ready schools: A report of the Goal 1 Ready Schools Resource Group.* Washington, DC: The National Education Goals Panel.

Spence-Babcock, S. (1995). Early childhood programs in other nations: Goals and outcomes. *The Future of Children, 5*(3), 94-114.

Stipek, D. (2004). Teaching practices in kindergarten and first grade: Different strokes for different folks. *Early Childhood Research Quarterly, 19,* 548-568.

Stipek, D. J., Feiler, R., Byler, P., Ryan, S., Milburn, S., & Salmon, J. M. (1998). Good beginnings: What difference does the program make in preparing young children for school? *Journal of Applied Developmental Psychology, 19*(1), 41-66.

Timmons, J. C., McIntyre, J. P., Whitney-Thomas, J., Butterworth, J., & Allen, D. (1998). Barriers to transition planning for parents of adolescents with special health care needs. *Research to Practice, 4*(7), 1-2.

Troup, K. S., & Malone, D. M. (2002). Transitioning preschool children with developmental concerns into kindergarten: Ecological characteristics of inclusive kindergarten programs. *Journal of Developmental and Physical Disabilities, 14*(4), 339-352.

Tudge, J. R. H., Odero, D. A., Hogan, D. M., & Etz, K. E. (2003). Relations between the everyday activities of preschoolers and their teachers' perceptions of their competence in the first years of school. *Early Childhood Research Quarterly, 18,* 42–64.

Wagner, M. M., & Blackorby, J. (1996). Transition from high school to work or college: How special education students fare. *The Future of Children, 6*(1), 103-120.

Ward, B. A., Mergendoller, J. R., & Tikunoff, W. J. (1982). Effects of instructional organization on students' transition success. *Journal of Early Adolescence, 2*(4), 339-365.

White, P. H., Edelman, A., & Schuyler, V. (2001). Success on the road to adulthood. In M. L. Batshaw (Ed.), *When your child has a disability: The complete sourcebook of daily and medical care* (pp. 425-434). Baltimore: Paul H. Brookes.

Wigfield, A., & Eccles, J. S. (1994). Children's competence beliefs, achievement values, and general self esteem change across elementary and middle school. *Journal of Early Adolescence, 14*(2), 107-138.

Wigfield, A., Eccles, J. S., MacIver, D., Reuman, D. A., & Midgley, C. (1991). Transitions during early adolescence: Changes in children's domain specific self-perceptions and general self-esteem across the transition to junior high school. *Developmental Psychology, 27,* 552–565.

Wolery, M. (1989). Transitions in early childhood special education: Issues and procedures. *Focus on Exceptional Children, 22*(2), 1-16.

Wood, S. J., & Cronnin, M. E. (1999). Students with emotional/behavioral disorders and transition planning: What the follow-up studies tell us. *Psychology in the Schools, 36*(4), 327-335.

Zeedyk, M. S., Gallacher, J., Henderson, M., Hope, G., Husband, B., & Lindsay, K. (2003). Negotiating the transition from primary to secondary school: Perceptions of pupils, parents and teachers. *School Psychology International, 24*(1), 67-79.

Zill, N. (1999). Promoting educational equity and excellence in kindergarten. In R. C. Pianta & M. J. Cox (Eds.), *The transition to kindergarten* (pp. 67-105). Baltimore: Paul H. Brookes.

Zill, N., & West, J. (2001). *Entering kindergarten: A portrait of American children when they begin school—Findings from the condition of education 2000.* (U.S. Department of Education, National Center for Education Statistics, NCES 2001–035). Washington, DC: U.S. Government Printing Office.

## Case Study

*Think back to Julianne's experiences in school when answering the questions below.*

## Questions

1. Should curriculum expectations be lowered because a student with a mild intellectual disability and cerebral palsy is in a 1st-grade special education classroom? Why or why not? What curriculum accommodations might you suggest for Julianne at this grade level that would allow her to learn the same 1st-grade curriculum, in the general education classroom, as her peers who are non-disabled?

2. How might you assist and lend support to Julianne's parents (i.e., as Julianne becomes older), who are now spending more time at home keeping her academically on track with her peers who are non-disabled?

3. Create a time line that clearly delineates the educational support and services that were given to Julianne and her parents from birth to adulthood. Add an additional layer of possible supports and services that might have further assisted Julianne academically and socially. Consider what new skills Julianne might need to learn. Who would teach her these skills? What new supports should be put into place? How might this be accomplished?

4. How might a "circle of friends" assist Julianne both academically and socially during a crucial period of time? (Refer to each critical transitional period.)

# Chapter 10

# Assistive Technology

*Gail Teachman, Cynthia Tam, and Jennifer Mays*

*Jason is a Grade 5 student who has weak fine motor skills and uses limited speech for communication. He is able to color and write on "fill in the blank" worksheets by using a slant board at his desk and a pencil or marker with a pencil grip. He finds it helpful to use manipulatives and a magnetic board for literacy and numeracy activities. It is important that Jason have good posture—as much as possible—while seated at his desk, which means his elbows are at desk height, feet resting securely on the floor. His classroom team assists him in using a graphic symbol set that augments his understanding of classroom activities and helps clarify his attempts at speech. These symbols also are placed prominently around the classroom and embedded within curriculum materials to increase the amount of visual cues available for Jason. He carries with him a small, personalized binder of communication symbols for communicating with others. Before he was introduced to Picture Communication Symbols (PCS), he used photographs to help represent language. Jason is just beginning to read, and he particularly enjoys electronic storybooks with text-to-speech technology.*

*Arianna is a 12-year-old girl with cerebral palsy who does not speak. She uses a power wheelchair, which she controls by hitting a sequence of switches mounted on the chair's headrest. When Arianna is not driving, she uses these same switches to access her dynamic screen, voice output communication aid (VOCA). Her device is a Dynavox, which is mounted where she can see the screen easily, on a heavy metal bar on her wheelchair. Arianna hits her switch to start the device, which then scans across pages on the screen, lighting up each choice in a pre-set pattern. When it scans to the one she wants, Arianna hits the switch again and the device speaks her selection aloud. The Dynavox is her voice as well as a writing tool. She uses it to communicate with her educational assistant, her teacher, and her peers, as well as to complete many writing activities (journal, spelling, even some math activities).*

*Arianna has used many different VOCAs during her elementary school years. She used to use picture communication symbols (PCS) along with text for all of her messages; as her literacy skills have developed, she has moved to working with text only. For some school subjects, Arianna wheels over to her desktop computer station, where, using an infrared signal, she is able to send information from her Dynavox to her desktop screen. She starts many writing projects this way. She also uses her switches and adaptive software to control a reading software program, Kurzweil 3000. The program gives Arianna access to classroom textbooks along with many E-books. She loves the* Anne of Green Gables *series!*

A bout a decade ago, Janice Light, a leading investigator in the fields of education and disability, made the following comment: "Technology is a tool . . . not the end goal itself" (Light, 1997). In keeping with this statement, this chapter will introduce the concept of assistive technology and provide examples to highlight the *enabling* role of assistive technology (AT) in the classroom.

## Defining Assistive Technology (AT)

In an inclusive classroom, students with physical and or communication disabilities may confront barriers to completing typical school tasks. A student with mobility impairments may be a strong reader but encounter years of frustration while struggling to become a writer. For these students, the educational and rehabilitation fields have developed an ever-growing range of assistive technologies. The term "assistive technology," which developed in the field of rehabilitation, describes devices and materials that help individuals with disabilities improve their ability to participate successfully within various occupations and environments. The terms "adaptive technology" or "assistive devices" may also be used; we use the term "assistive technology," as we find it the most inclusive and the most internationally prevalent term.

AT literature abounds with various and inconsistent definitions for subcategories or types of assistive technology. Perhaps most commonly used are the terms "low tech" and "high tech." Although ill-defined, these terms will be used here to introduce some of the vast array of AT devices that may enable students to participate more fully in the classroom. "Low-tech" devices are usually described as inexpensive, readily available, and non-electronic, or even homemade (e.g., a rubber pencil grip, a clipboard, or adapted scissors). "High-tech" solutions and devices generally involve more expensive, electronic, or computer-based hardware and software solutions.

One problem arising from the common use of these terms is that it is often perceived that expensive high-tech solutions must be better than relatively inexpensive low-tech solutions; however, there is no evidence to support or refute this assumption. There *is* strong, compelling evidence that a good fit (i.e., a careful match of the user and the task to the technology) will be most successful. A number of recent reviews of AT use in the classroom have addressed the efficacy of technology for students with disabilities (Fitzgerald & Koury, 1996; Shiah, Mastropieri, & Scruggs, 1995; Woodward & Rieth, 1997). Each bears out this critical variable of "good fit" in ensuring that the use of AT will increase the likelihood that students can participate in school activities.

An AT assessment that considers the student's skills may be initiated by a therapist (e.g., an occupational, physical, or speech-language therapist). This assessment also should consider the variety of tasks (needs) and the inherent supports and barriers that may exist in the classroom environment for that student. In order to match assistive technology with the student, pros and cons must be considered carefully by the classroom team, the student, and his or her family. For example, some high-tech communication devices are very expensive, cumbersome, and complex; yet, these same devices offer the potential to increase a student's ability to communicate across various environments, enhance his participation in school life, and yield a positive psychosocial impact. A student's individual needs are likely to change frequently as school activities change, as the student matures, and as the school environment changes. This means that the match of AT with the student must be reevaluated on an ongoing basis. Generally, the most successful applications of AT are those that provide a student with a variety of AT options, both low and high tech, to accommodate the wide variety of tasks, settings, and activities found within a busy school day.

## Frameworks for Assistive Technology

A variety of frameworks are available to guide AT assessment and implementation in a classroom setting. Most educators will find the SETT Framework (Student, Environment, Tasks, Tools) (Zabala, 1995) to be a relevant and meaningful guide. This framework was developed by an educator, Joy Smiley Zabala, working with the Wisconsin Assistive Technology Initiative. SETT calls for a team to assess, implement, evaluate, and adjust the use of AT in classrooms by posing a variety of questions, such as: What does the student need to do? What are the student's current skills and abilities? What supports are available to the student and the partners? What materials and equipment are available? What system of tools does this student need to perform these tasks in these environments? How might the tools be tried out in natural environments? The SETT Framework honors all perspectives and provides a common language to unite often diverse teams. In so doing, it provides an extremely valuable tool.

Several other models reinforce the same critical factors stressed in the SETT model and could be used to guide the process of selecting AT. A framework from the World Health Organization (WHO), the International Classification of Functioning, Disability and Health (ICF) (WHO, 2002), stresses the need to consider activities and participation as they occur within a specific context. The Matching Person and Technology Model (MPT) (Scherer, 1994) stresses the importance of the client's personal characteristics and values in determining which technologies may be a match for that person in his or her environment and in evaluating the effectiveness of that match.

The Canadian Model of Occupational Performance (CMOP) (Canadian Association of Occupational Therapists, 1997) is based on the belief that the person is central and integral to the process of setting therapeutic goals and measuring outcomes. The Person-Environment-Occupation Model (PEO) (Law et al., 1996) further describes how this dynamic conceptualization of the individual, the environment, and occupational performance can be applied (Strong et al., 1999).

In each of these models, disability is viewed not as the sum of a person's performance limitations. Rather, it is determined by the individual's perception of how those limitations have affected her ability to participate in selected occupations within her environment (Baum & Law, 1997; Ripat, Etcheverry, Cooper, & Tate, 2001).

What follows is a selective overview of devices commonly introduced into school settings, described with a view to identifying for the reader which students may benefit from which types of AT. Case profiles are used to illustrate how AT has enabled students to succeed and enjoy the shared experience of learning; these profiles also demonstrate the need for assessment to be ongoing, as students' needs will change over time.

So many options are available within various types of AT that it would not be feasible to undertake a comprehensive review here. Throughout this chapter, specific product names have been provided as examples, not as recommendations. Just as in other technology fields, products and availabilities change quickly and tend to vary greatly by geography. We have endeavored to select examples where more information about this type of product can be found on Web sites (see Tables 1 and 2).

## Low-Tech Devices

When considering assistive technology for a student, low-tech strategies should be considered before high-tech solutions (Blackhurst, 1997). Because low-tech devices are often inexpensive and do not require extensive training to implement, a classroom teacher may begin exploring low-tech options independently or with the aid of a therapist or technology team. The LoTTIE (Low Tech Tools for Inclusive Education) Kit is an example of a commercially available collection of low-tech tools for educators to begin trying different low-tech solutions with students. The LoTTIE is available from Onion Mountain Technology Inc. (www.onionmountaintech.com/) (Product Spotlight, 2003).

### Writing

Difficulty with handwriting remains the most common reason why a student is referred to a school-based occupational therapist (Amundson, 2001). Fortunately, many low-tech devices exist that can help students with handwriting difficulties. A student with physical impairment must be seated properly in order to effectively write. If a chair or table is too high or low, it may be difficult for the student to use any tools for writing. An adjustable-height desk (e.g., Idea Cart, Single Surface Adjustable Computer Workstation) and an adjustable-height chair (e.g., Tripp Trapp Chair, Kinder Chair) will enable the student to be seated appropriately and can accommodate the student as he or she grows. Footrests, or a small footstool or phone book, can provide foot support; however, with a proper height-adjustable chair and desk, footrests should not be necessary. An adjustable slant board or easel placed on the desk can enable the student to position the paper at a comfortable angle. Non-slip mats, such as Dycem, can be placed on the desk or slant board if the student is having difficulty stabilizing manipulatives or other low-tech tools on the desk.

Some students may have difficulty stabilizing the paper on the desk. If this is the case, the paper can be taped to the desk, placed on a clipboard, or held down with sticky tack. Try an adapted pen or pencil for the student who has difficulty holding a regular pencil; pencil grips also may make it easier. Modeling clay can be used to create a custom pencil grip for a student. In addition, pens and pencils of various thicknesses, shapes, and weights are available commercially in most school and office supply stores. Markers or ink pens may be easier for a student to use, as they require less pressure. Softer or harder pencils are identified by the HB value stamped on the pencil. A harder pencil lead will produce a lighter line, so this choice may be appropriate for a child who presses the pencil to the paper very forcefully. A softer pencil lead will produce a darker line, so it may be helpful for the student who presses very lightly. Tactile letters (felt, magnetic, cards) or rubber stamps (name stamp, letter or number stamps) can be used to form words and sentences if the child is unable to use a pencil or pen. A cookie sheet can be used as an inexpensive magnetic board for magnetic letters or words (Newton, Case, & Bauder, 2002). Special paper with extra lines, embossed or raised lines, or larger spacing between the lines may enable a student with handwriting difficulties to produce text that is more legible.

Often, a student who has difficulty with handwriting will benefit from having a teacher provide copies of notes before the lesson. This practice allows the student to focus on the content of the lesson, rather than on the physical skills required to copy text. Highlighter pens or highlighter tape can help the student develop note-taking skills. Post-it

Notes also may be useful to excerpt important ideas from a passage. Although recording a lesson with a tape recorder with a counter can assist some older students, this strategy is very time-consuming if someone also must transcribe the notes. Recordings are more useful as an auditory record of the lesson that students can listen to repeatedly and from which they can extract important short notations.

For students with learning disabilities, electronic dictionaries (such as the Speaking Language Master, Speaking Homework Wiz, and the Speaking Spelling and Handwriting Ace) may be helpful (Assistive Technology Training Online Project [ATTO], n.d.). These small portable devices can help a student look up a word using phonetic spelling, provide pronunciation, and provide a definition to ensure that the student selects the correct word.

## Reading

A student with poor motor control, sensory motor delays, or vision impairment may have trouble reading. Books can be adapted with symbols above words. Or, using a ruler, reading ruler, word window, or line marker may enable the student to follow a line of text more easily. Large-print books may be easier to read for students with physical or visual difficulties. Photocopies of the words from a classroom "word wall," placed in pockets on the wall, enable students to bring the word card to their desk for practice.

Book holders (e.g., Roberts Book Holder or the Book Butler) can be useful for students who cannot hold a book or turn the page independently. Pencil erasers or rubber tipped hand-held or mouth pointers could be used to turn pages. For even more assistance in turning pages, tabs (such as popsicle sticks) or spacers (a small piece of sponge, a dot of glue, or a small piece of felt) that are glued between the pages of a picture book may allow the student to turn pages independently. Different types of paper can be easier to turn; when making books in the classroom, it is helpful to use thicker paper, like card stock (Newton, Case, & Bauder, 2002). Some electronic page turners are available (e.g., Touch Turner) for use with a single switch (ATTO, n.d.).

## Across the Curriculum

A student who requires low-technology devices will benefit from access to these tools across all subject areas. For example, in geography class, a textured map or sticker labels can make coloring and labeling more efficient. In science class, microscopes can be placed on a lower table for a wheelchair user; chemistry tools can be built up, using foam to make gripping easier; nets can be used to assist in collecting specimens (Peterson, 1995). During an art lesson, adapted scissors (e.g., Mary Benbow scissors, Softgrip pointed scissors, Loop Spring scissors, or Squeezzers) can enable a child with fine motor difficulties to cut independently (ATTO, n.d.). Paper punches also can be used to enable students to cut out various shapes independently. Many different types of markers may be easier to use than pencils; rubber stamps can enable students to create pictures. Adapted paint brushes or crayons and magnet board shape sets can help students to create patterns or designs. Hardened glue along the lines of a coloring page may enable a student to stay within the lines.

A student with fine motor difficulties may have trouble lining up numbers on paper to do calculations. Graph paper provides a useful visual guide for this task; paper with raised lines provides tactile cues. An abacus or other manipulatives, such as MathLine, and containers for sorting may help with counting and calculations. Calculators can enable a student to do basic calculations, count money, graph, or learn to work with fractions (Coin-U-Lator, Calc-U-Vue, Texas Instruments Elementary Calculator TI-108, Casio Fraction Mate FX-55) (ATTO, n.d.).

## Communication and Participation

Some students have difficulties with face-to-face communication (i.e., they are non-speaking or experience significant difficulty with speech). These students often benefit from using augmentative or alternate communication (AAC) strategies. These tools and strategies facilitate the representation of language to make choices, communicate wants and needs, and increase interaction with peers. Communication books or displays can be created that use symbol sets, such as concrete objects, photographs, graphic symbol sets, letters, words, or phrases (Center for Special Education Technology, 1990). Pictures can be placed around the classroom and made into theme displays for particular activities. Visual schedules created from symbols can help a student who has difficulty with transitions. The Go! Board system is an example of a low-tech visual schedule, in a vertical arrangement with a pocket at the bottom for storing completed activities. A "first: then" display board can provide structure for students who must complete one activity before starting a more desired activity. These same symbols or pictures also can be used on an electronic voice output communication aid (VOCA), such as Big Mack Communicator, Step-by-Step Communicator (Big or Little), Twin Talk, Go Talk, or CheapTalk. This type of low-tech communication device may enable a student to signal for attention, participate in calendar time, initiate requests, or greet friends. For a student who is unable to raise his or her hand in class, or who is unable to call for attention, other signaling devices may be used, such as a buzzer, chime, or a tape-recorded message (Center for Special Education Technology, 1990).

Some students with severely limited use of their hands and arms will benefit from using an electronic switch to control high- or low-tech devices. Usually, an occupational therapist needs to complete an assessment in order to recommend the best site for using a switch. Students with limited physical mobility may use a hand, finger, head, foot, knee, elbow, chin, eye blink, or any other voluntary movement to activate a switch. Many different types of switches are available and they can be used singly or in multiples, depending on the device being accessed. Switches often are introduced early to facilitate control of battery-operated toys for children who cannot otherwise manipulate toys. A switch latch and timer can be used together with a switch to add functionality. For example, in latch mode, the switch will operate like an on/off switch. In the timer mode, the switch will turn the device on for a set amount of time. An adapter device, such as the Power Link 3 by AbleNet, can allow switch users to control such electrical appliances as a fan, light, blender, page turner, or tape recorder. Switches are also frequently used to provide access to simple VOCAs or signaling devices.

Instructions can be found on the Internet to create a homemade low-tech type of switch (e.g., a Mouse in a House) to access a high-tech device such as the computer.

## Organization

Organizational skills are critical to a student's academic success. Students can improve upon their organizational skills through such low-tech strategies as making flow charts, task analysis, webbing, and outlining (Behrmann & Jerome, 2002).

## TABLE 1: WEB SITES FOR INFORMATION ON LOW-TECH SOLUTIONS

| Devices/Software | Web Sites |
|---|---|
| **Adjustable-Height Desks**<br>Idea Cart<br>Single Surface Adjustable Computer Work-station, Adjustable Desk,<br>Personal Worktable | www.anthro.com<br>www.sammonspreston.com |
| **Height-Adjustable Chairs**<br>Tripp Trapp chair<br>(also called STOKKE KinderZeat)<br>Kinder Chair | www.stokke.com<br><br>www.sammonspreston.com<br>www.kayeproducts.com |
| **Slant Boards/Tabletop Easels**<br>SiDiKi Portable Transparent Writing/<br>Activities Table | www.otideas.com<br>www.theraproducts.com<br>www.sammonspreston.com |
| **Non-slip Surface Material**<br>Dycem | www.dycem.com |
| **Pencil Grips** | www.theraproducts.com<br>www.sammonspreston.com<br>www.otideas.com |
| **Adapted Pencils and Pens**<br>Triangular pencils, pens, crayons<br>Weighted pens | www.theraproducts.com<br>www.sammonspreston.com |
| **Adapted Writing Paper**<br>Raised Line Paper<br>Hint Print paper<br>Smart Start paper | www.theraproducts.com<br>www.otideas.com<br>www.theraproducts.com |
| **Highlighter Tape** | www.leeproducts.com<br>www.trcabc.com |
| **Small Electronic Aids**<br>Speaking Language Master<br>Speaking Homework Wiz<br>Speaking Spelling and Handwriting<br>Ace | www.franklin.com |
| **Reading Ruler** | www.crossboweducation.com |
| **Book Holders**<br>Roberts Book Holder<br>Book Butler | www.theraproducts.com<br>www.sammonspreston.com |
| **Rubber Tipped Hand, Head, and Mouth Pointers** | www.sammonspreston.com |
| **Touch Turner** | www.touchturner.com |
| **Graphic Symbol Sets**<br>Mayer Johnson Picture Communication Symbols (PCS) | www.mayer-johnson.com |
| **Visual Schedules**<br>Go! Board System | www.enablingdevices.com |

| | |
|---|---|
| **Simple Voice Output Devices**<br>Big Mack Communicator<br>Sequencer<br>Step-by-Step Communicator (Big or Little)<br>Go Talk<br>6 Level Communicator<br>Twin Talk<br>CheapTalk<br>Macaw | www.ablenetinc.com<br>www.adaptive-sol.com<br>www.ablenetinc.com<br>www.attainmentcompany.com<br>www.sammonspreston.com<br>www.enablingdevices.com<br>www.enablingdevices.com<br>www.zygo-usa.com |
| **Scissors**<br>Benbow Scissors<br>Loop Scissors | www.fiskars.com<br>www.theraproducts.com |
| **Paper Punches** | www.fiskars.com |
| **MathLine** | www.howbrite.com |
| **Coin-U-Lator** | www.attainmentcompany.com |
| **Calc-U-Vue** | www.learningresources.com |
| **Texas Instruments Elementary Calculator TI-108** | http://education.ti.com/us/product/tech/108/features/features.html |
| **Fraction Mate FX-55 by Casio** | www.casio.com |
| **Switches** (commercial and homemade)<br>Jelly Bean® switches<br>Big Red® switch<br>Homemade switch<br>Mouse House by Linda Burkhart | www.ablenetinc.com<br>www.sammonspreston.com; www.ablenetinc.com<br>www.ataccess.org/resources/wcp/enswitches/enmaking.html<br>www.lburkhart.com/mhouse.htm |
| **Switch-Adapted Toys** | www.sammonspreston.com<br>www.flaghouse.com |
| **Switch Latch and Timer** | www.ablenetinc.com<br>www.sammonspreston.com |
| **Adaptor Cables** (commercial & homemade) | www.ablenetinc.com<br>www.ataccess.org/resources/wep/enswitches/enadapting<br>toy.html |
| **Power Link 3® Control Unit Set** | www.ablenetinc.com<br>www.sammonspreston.com |

## High-Tech Devices

Many high-tech devices can be helpful to students with disabilities. Since a great variety of products are available and many are complex and costly, a multidisciplinary team should select the most appropriate device for the student, the task, and the environment.

## Access Considerations

With regard to high-tech devices, a misconception often exists that the more expensive, complicated solution is a better solution. When deciding on an appropriate access method for a student, however, the use of a standard keyboard and a standard mouse with minor adaptations, for example, should be considered before trying out high-tech alternatives. Wherever feasible, the ability to use standard equipment enables students to gain access in more settings—at school, in public libraries, at a friend's home, or at work/study.

*Keyboard.* The keyboard responses on a standard computer or a computer-based device can be modified to help the student (see Accessibility Options, Table 2). For a student who types with one finger, employing the StickyKeys option allows the student to type a capitalized letter or hotkey combination (e.g., control + P for printing) without the need to hold down both keys at the same time. StickyKeys allows these keys to be pressed in sequence. In another example, pressing the "Shift" key followed by a letter key would type a capitalized letter. Other features of the keyboard, such as the repeat rate and key sensitivity, also can be adjusted to support students with a slight tremor or with too heavy a touch on the keyboard.

Alternative keyboards are available for students who cannot use a standard keyboard because of reduced coordination or limited strength and range in the upper limbs. A larger keyboard (e.g., IntelliKeys) may be helpful to a student who has difficulty accurately targeting the keys on a standard keyboard. A smaller keyboard (e.g., a Sejin keyboard) accommodates for reduced range of movement. Keyboards that can be split in the middle and set in any desired angle (e.g., the Comfort Keyboard System) are necessary for students who need to type with their wrists in certain positions. Some keyboards (e.g., the TASH mini-keyboard) are called "membrane keyboards." These keyboards are touch-sensitive and do not require any strength to press the keys. When a physical keyboard is not possible, an on-screen keyboard that can be activated with a mouse or a mouse alternative can be considered (e.g., WiVik3).

*Mouse.* The ability to relate and control movement of a mouse as it relates to movement of the mouse cursor on a monitor may be very challenging for young children, with or without physical difficulties. It is particularly difficult for children with motor or perceptual deficits. Simple adjustments to the speed or size of the mouse cursor on the screen can be made through the mouse control settings. Another setting within Accessibility Options allows a student to control the mouse by using the keyboard's arrow keys.

Instead of a mouse, some students use a trackball (e.g., Kensington Expert Mouse). Trackballs require a different type of physical task to control the cursor and they usually offer separate control of the movement of the mouse cursor and the clicking of a button to select a target. Trackballs are often helpful to students who have difficulty gripping a mouse and who inadvertently move the cursor off their target when they try to click. Trackpads, frequently seen on laptop computers, are activated by sliding a finger across the pad (e.g., the Cirque Easy Cat) and serve as an alternative to the mouse. Students who experience ataxia, an inability to control movements, may find a joystick easier to control than a trackball (e.g., the Penny and Giles Joystick). A student who has no functional use of her hands may need to use an infrared head-pointing mouse (e.g., the HeadMouse) or a switch-controlled mouse (e.g., the TASH Mouse Interface 5).

*Speech Recognition.* Speech recognition is computer software (e.g., NaturallySpeaking, ViaVoice) that lets people control a computer by speaking into it via a microphone connected to the computer. By speaking into the computer, users can "type" words into standard word processing applications. They also can control many computer applications by saying the appropriate commands. Speech recognition has the potential to be very helpful to students with disabilities, but the steps involved in using the software are very complex. Therefore, it is not suitable for everybody. A certain level of reading ability, good spelling skills, strong cognitive skills, motivation for writing, and a solid foundation in the use of a computer for writing are required in order to use speech recognition successfully and independently. Koester (2004) found that although people can speak at a rate of 110-120 words per minute, use of speech recognition does not generate text at an equally fast rate. The range of text generation rate reported was between 3-32 words per minute (M=16.9). Being able to consistently follow correction strategies is the key to success in the use of speech recognition.

*Text-to-Speech (also known as auditory feedback or speech synthesis).* Text-to-speech software programs (e.g., IntelliTalk 3; Write: Outloud) provide audio feedback of the letters, words, sentences, and/or paragraphs as a student types. Research indicates that text-to-speech technology allows students with learning disabilities to use their general language sense to monitor their writing, and catch errors in grammar, spelling, and punctuation (Hunt-Berg, Ranking, & Beukelman, 1994). Williams (2002) reported that when students with learning disabilities use text-to-speech software to produce writing, they write more independently and with better quality. They were also more interested in writing.

*Word Prediction.* Word prediction technology (e.g., WordQ, Co: Writer) monitors the keys that the user types and generates a list of the most likely words and displays them in a prediction list. The user then selects the desired word from the prediction list by pressing a designated key on the keyboard, usually a number key. Thus, the user does not have to type each individual letter of the word. Word prediction computer software was developed to increase the rate of text entry for individuals with physical disabilities. However, some studies have found no difference in the rate of text entry with or without word prediction, while some researchers reported lower rates with word prediction (Anson, 1993; Tam, Reid, O'Keefe, & Naumann, 2002). On the other hand, when used with students with learning disabilities, word prediction has been found to have the potential to improve spelling and increase the variety of words used in compositions (Handley-More, Deitz, Billingsley, & Coggins, 2003). Word cueing is a relatively new term that refers to technology that combines word prediction and text-to-speech technology. Word cueing incorporates the new research on natural language processing to make the prediction more relevant to the student's own vocabulary. It has been found to be very helpful to students with learning difficulties (Tam, Mays, Archer, & Skidmore, 2004).

## Writing Strategies

Difficulties in writing could occur at any or all stages of writing, from generating ideas to composing and editing. Outlining and semantic webbing are common practices for organizing ideas before writing. Inspiration or Kidspiration software can help students with brainstorming, webbing, and organizing their ideas. Students can insert notes related to each idea. They also can work in outline format and transfer the outline to standard word-processing software, such as Microsoft Word, for composing and editing purposes. Some word prediction software and text-to-speech software can be used within Inspiration. Inspiration also provides limited text-to-speech support. In the composing and editing stage, students can continue to use word prediction or word cueing software to help them with the mechanical aspect of writing (e.g., spelling, punctuation, and capitalization).

The education community is becoming increasingly aware of the benefits provided by multimedia software (MacArthur, 2000). Multimedia software programs provide integrated drawing tools, clip art, and sound effects along with limited text capabilities (e.g., KidPix

Deluxe 3). Programs such as IntelliTalk 3 go one step further. In addition to providing multimedia capabilities, IntelliTalk 3 supports custom-made word banks and provides word prediction. Multimedia software can be used to motivate students to write and they compensate for weak basic skills. For example, Amazing Writing Machine provides templates and sample projects for students with writing difficulties. It also incorporates sound and pictures, thereby encouraging creativity and motivating young students to write.

Having access to appropriate word-processing software is essential for writing on the computer. Generally speaking, students who use their own computers for writing at school should use the same word-processing software as the rest of their classmates. This helps to remove or reduce the sense of being different and, more important, facilitates sharing of information among students for group work and transferring of files between home and school. Standard word-processing software (e.g., Word, WordPerfect) includes features that help students with disabilities to write more efficiently. For example, the Auto-Correct feature in Microsoft Word can be used for a technique that is called "abbreviation expansion" where, for example, the software can easily be programmed to type "Yours truly" when the student types "yt."

Students with writing difficulties often struggle with writing within the small spaces provided on a worksheet. Software that supports the use of a scanner and optical character recognition (OCR), like Kurzweil 3000, can be used to change the worksheet into an electronic text file so that students can type their answers right into the worksheet. Simple scanning tools, such as Microsoft Office Document Imaging, can be used to scan the worksheet and present it in a graphic format. Students then can fill in the blanks, using the textbox tool. The Form Tool on standard word-processing software also can easily create worksheets. IntelliTalk 3 provides a locked text function—students working with the locked worksheet can type in the blank spots while the original text is protected.

Students who use alternate symbol sets for some or all of their writing can use software that integrates traditional text with symbols or pictures. They can access this software in a variety of alternative formats (e.g., using an on-screen grid or using a single switch to select a word or symbol). IntelliTalk 3, Clicker 5, and Writing with Symbols are all examples of this type of writing software.

*Portable Devices.* The use of a computer for writing offers relief for students who have difficulty with pencil and paper tasks. Portable writing devices are often necessary to meet the needs of such students in the classroom. Many dedicated word processors (e.g., Dana, Neo, and Laser PC6) are available. These devices are lightweight and easy to operate, but limited to word-processing functions. They typically provide basic word-processing and spell-checking functions, and possibly a thesaurus and a calculator. Additional functions are being added to these devices to support students with disabilities. The Neo is shipped with Co: Writer. Dana doubles as a palm device. The pre-loaded software on the Dana include the compact versions of Inspiration and Write: Outloud. The Laser PC6 also can provide text-to-speech capability. The choice between a word processor and a portable computer depends on the student's needs. If the availability of a wide range of software is required or the student requires the use of an adapted keyboard, then a portable computer is necessary. However, a portable computer poses a higher security risk, is heavy yet less rugged, and is more limited in the number of hours that it will run continuously on battery power.

Portable equipment can provide useful assistance to memory and organization skills. Portable digital assistant (PDA) devices, such as the Palm and Pocket PC, include such features as Sticky Notes and Bookmarks that serve as memory aids. All PDAs have scheduling software, along with an address and phone book, to prompt both memory and organization. There is increasing availability of compact versions of software (e.g., a Pocket PC version of Microsoft Office for use with PDAs). This makes it possible for these devices to be used as portable writing devices. The use of a foldable keyboard (e.g., the Cyberhand keyboard), attached to the PDA, increases efficiency and ease of use for this function.

*Note-taking.* The task of note-taking is very often challenging for students with disabilities related to physical and learning factors. However, note-taking is not an area where technology has been shown to offer much assistance. Being able to type and listen at the same time requires a high level of integrated typing, listening, and language skills. In our experience, this is not feasible for most students with physical disabilities. Instead, accommodations, such as assigning a designated note-taker, providing scribe assistance, and arranging for a copy of notes from peers or teachers, are usually better options. Newer software programs such as OneNote, a recent addition to Microsoft Office, do offer opportunities for students to develop their note-taking skills and to import and edit notes taken by other students or from Web resources.

*Reading.* Many electronic books (E-books) can be downloaded from the Internet for a small fee or for free. Classroom texts can be scanned and read by a student independently by using such software as Scan and Read, Kurzweil 3000, or free shareware. E-books can be read on a computer with text-to-speech software, on a Pocket PC or Palm, or on portable E-book devices (e.g., Franklin, E-Book). E-books often highlight the text as the book is read. Books on tape or videos also can be useful. Electronic word walls can be created for students who require the additional support of text-to-speech features, symbol support, or single switch access.

## Math and Science
Students with writing difficulties often struggle with writing math and science symbols and equations. For example, they are not able to write numbers in the proper columns. Such software as MathPad assists students in the junior grades to format and write math equations on the computer. Young students who have difficulties with handling manipulatives could use such software programs as Intellimathics, which simulates this learning tool on-screen. For high school students, the Equation Editor that is included in Microsoft Word or WordPerfect would allow them to type math equations. For more sophisticated equations and symbols, they could use such software programs as MathType and Scientific Notebook. However, writing equations this way demands very good mouse skills, which is often a challenge for students with physical disabilities. MathTalk, a software program that sends NaturallySpeaking commands into MathPad or Scientific Notebook, allows students to dictate their math work.

## Communication and Participation
Many types of high-tech voice output devices are available for students who have severely limited speech function. Multi-message and multi-level devices allow a word or phrase to

be recorded for a series of "buttons" that have PCS and text labels applied to the coordinating message buttons. These devices are in a mid-range for both cost and weight. They tend to be easily portable and the messages can be changed and updated frequently. The major limitation of these devices is that a limited amount of vocabulary can be stored and accessed. An example of this type of device is the Chat Box, an introductory augmentative communication aid that uses a unique symbol set—the Minspeak visual language system—for storage and retrieval of messages.

In order to allow access to a much greater variety of vocabulary and in order to organize the words and phrases, dynamic screen devices house a computer within a heavy-duty case, along with complex, adaptive software. These larger, heavier, and very costly VOCAs usually feature synthesized and digitized speech, computer emulation, and infrared environmental controls. Dynavox (DV4), Mercury, and Vanguard Plus are examples of this type of device. It takes time and training for students and their school teams to implement these tools successfully, but the potential for supporting communication competence, appropriate socialization opportunities, and school success makes this high investment worthwhile.

TABLE 2: WEB SITES FOR INFORMATION ON HIGH-TECH DEVICES

| Devices/Software | Web Sites |
| --- | --- |
| **Accessibility Options**<br>Macintosh<br>Windows | www.apple.com/accessibility<br>www.microsoft.com/enable |
| **Alternative Keyboards**<br>IntelliKeys<br>Sejin mini keyboard<br>Comfort keyboard system<br>TASH mini<br>WiViK3 | www.intellitools.com<br>www.sejin.com<br>www.ergocanada.com<br>www.tashinc.com<br>www.wivik.com |
| **Alternative Mouse**<br>Kensington Expert Mouse<br>Cirque Easy Cat<br>Penny & Giles joystick<br>HeadMouse<br>TASH Interface 5 | www.kensington.com<br>www.cirque.com<br>www.donjohnston.com/catalog/pengild.htm<br>www.orin.com<br>www.tashinc.com |
| **Speech Recognition**<br>NaturallySpeaking<br>ViaVoice | www.scansoft.com<br>www.nuance.com |
| **Text-to-Speech**<br>IntelliTalk 3<br>Write: Outloud | www.intellitools.com<br>www.donjohnston.com |
| **Word Prediction**<br>WordQ<br>Co:Writer | www.wordq.com<br>www.donjohnston.com |
| **Multi-message VOCAs**<br>ChatBox<br>Lightwriter | www.prentrom.com<br>www.zygo-usa.com/lighwrts.htm |

| | |
|---|---|
| **Dynamic VOCAs**<br>Vanguard<br>Dynavox<br>Mercury | www.prentrom.com<br>www.dynavoxtech.com<br>www.assistivetech.com/p-mercury.htm |
| **Writing Software**<br>Kid Pix Deluxe 3<br>Clicker 5<br>Writing with Symbols | www.broderbund.com<br>www.cricksoft.com<br>www.widgit.com/products/wws2000 |
| **Reading and Scanning**<br>Kurzweil 3000<br>Microsoft Office Document Imaging | www.kurzweiledu.com<br>http://office.microsoft.com/en-us/assistance<br>HP062193601033.aspx |
| **Portable Writing Devices**<br>Dana, Neo<br>Laser PC6<br>Cyberhand keyboard for PDA | www.alphasmart.com<br>www.perfectsolutions.com/pc6f.asp<br>www.pocketop.net |
| **Math and Science**<br>MathPad<br>IntelliMathics<br>MathType<br>Scientific Notebook<br>MathTalk | www.intellitools.com<br>www.intellitools.com<br>www.mathtype.com<br>www.mackichan.com<br>www.mathtalk.com |

## References

Amundson, S. J. (2001). Prewriting and handwriting skills. In J. Case-Smith (Ed.), *Occupational therapy for children* (pp. 545-568). St. Louis, MO: Mosby.

Anson, D. (1993). The effect of word prediction on typing speed. *American Journal of Occupational Therapy, 47*, 1039-1042.

Assistive Technology Training Online Project (ATTO). (n.d.). Retrieved December 21, 2004, from University of Buffalo School of Public Health and Health Professions Web site, http://atto.buffalo.edu

Baum, C. M., & Law, M. (1997). Occupational therapy practice: Focusing on occupational performance. *American Journal of Occupational Therapy, 51*(4), 277-288.

Behrmann, M., & Jerome, M. K. (2002). Assistive technology for students with mild disabilities: Update 2002. *ERIC Digest* E623. (ERIC Document Reproduction Service No. ED 463595)

Blackhurst, A. E. (1997). Perspectives on technology in special education. *Teaching Exceptional Children, 29*(5), 41-48.

Canadian Association of Occupational Therapists. (1997). *Enabling occupation: An occupational therapy perspective.* Ottawa, ON: Author.

Center for Special Education Technology. (1990). *Tech use guide. Using computer technology. Augmentative and alternative communication.* (Available from the Center for Special Education Technology, 1920 Association Drive, Reston, VA 22091)

Fitzgerald, G. E., & Koury, K. A. (1996). Empirical advances in technology-assisted instruction for students with mild and moderate disabilities. *Journal of Research on Computing in Education, 28*(4), 526-553.

Handley-More, D., Deitz, J., Billingsley, F. F., & Coggins, T. E. (2003). Facilitating written work using computer word processing and word prediction. *American Journal of Occupational Therapy, 57,* 139-151.

Hunt-Berg, M., Ranking, J. L., & Beukelman, D. R. (1994). Ponder the possibilities: Computer supported writing for struggling writers. *Learning Disabilities Research and Practice, 12*(3), 188-194.

Koester, H. (2004). Usage, performance, and satisfaction outcomes for experienced users of automatic speech recognition. *Journal of Rehabilitation Research & Development, 41*(5), 739-754.

Law, M., Cooper, B., Strong, S., Stewart, D., Rigby, P., & Letts, L. (1996). The Person-Environment-Occupation model: A transactive approach to occupational performance. *Canadian Journal of Occupational Therapy, 63,* 9-23.

Light, J. C. (1997). Communication is the essence of human life: Reflections on communicative competence. *Augmentative & Alternative Communication, 13,* 61-70.

MacArthur, C. A. (2000). New tools for writing: assistive technology for students with writing difficulties. *Topics in Language Disorders, 20*(4), 85-110.

Newton, D. A., Case, D. A., & Bauder, D. K. (2002). No- and low-tech tools to access the general curriculum. *Closing the Gap, 21*(4). Retrieved December 21, 2004, from www.closingthegap.com

Peterson, D. R. (1995, April). *The assessment of physical and program accessibility for students with physical (mobility) disabilities.* Paper presented at the Annual International Convention of the Council for Exceptional Children, Indianapolis, IN.

Product Spotlight. (2003). Low tech tool kits. *Closing the Gap, 21*(6). Retrieved December 21, 2004, from www.closingthegap.com

Ripat, J., Etcheverry, E., Cooper, J., & Tate, R. (2001). A comparison of the Canadian Occupational Performance Measure and the Health Assessment Questionnaire. *Canadian Journal of Occupational Therapy, 68*(4), 247-253.

Scherer, M. J. (1994). *Matching person and technology: A series of assessments for selecting and evaluating technologies used in rehabilitation, education, the workplace and other settings.* New York: Webster.

Shiah, R., Mastropieri, M. A., & Scruggs, T. E. (1995). Computer-assisted instruction and students with learning disabilities: Does research support the rhetoric? *Advances in Learning and Behavioral Disabilities, 9,* 162-192.

Strong, S., Rigby, P., Stewart, D., Law, M., Letts, L., & Cooper, B. (1999). Application of the Person-Environment-Occupation Model: A practical tool. *Canadian Journal of Occupational Therapy, 66,* 122-133.

Tam, C., Mays, J., Archer, J., & Skidmore, G. (2004). Effectiveness of word cueing for children with physical and learning disabilities. *Closing the Gap, 22*(5), 11, 12 & 23.

Tam, C., Reid, D., O'Keefe, B., & Naumann, S. (2002). Effects of word prediction and location of word prediction list on text entry with children with spina bifida and hydrocephalus. *Augmentative and Alternative Communication, 18,* 147-162.

Williams, S. C. (2002). How speech-feedback and word-prediction software can help students write. *Teaching Exceptional Children, 34*(3), 72-78.

Woodward, J., & Rieth, H. (1997). A historical review of technology research in special education. *Review of Educational Research, 67,* 503-536.

World Health Organization. (2002). *International classification of functioning, disability and health: Introduction.* Retrieved December 17, 2004, from www3.who.int/icf

Zabala, J. S. (1995). *The SETT Framework: Critical areas to consider when making informed assistive technology decisions.* Houston, TX: Region IV Education Service Center. (ERIC Document Reproduction Service No. ED 381962)

## Case Study

*James began to have difficulties with writing at the age of 12 because of Duchenne muscular dystrophy, a degenerative condition. While James was able to write at one time, weakness and fatigue related to writing gradually made it impossible for him to stay at this task for longer than 2 minutes at a time. Academically, James was progressing well. He began to rely on the use of a computer for writing. At this stage, he was able to use a standard computer keyboard and mouse.*

*About two years later, as James started to lose more strength and range of arm movements, he began to struggle when using a standard keyboard. A reduced-size, angled Sejin keyboard was introduced and James was able to use it for another couple of years. When James started to use his whole body to support his fingers to "crawl" up to the top row of the keyboard and to have difficulties reaching and holding the mouse, he switched to using a trackball with an on-screen keyboard to access the computer. Despite his physical challenges, James remained a competitive student. He was accepted into a general arts program at a local university. At the university and in an arts program, James found typing with the on-screen keyboard to be too slow to meet his writing needs. He explored the use of NaturallySpeaking, a speech recognition software. As a well-spoken, intelligent, and motivated user, James's speech was well-recognized by the software and he was able to devote time and energy to train the speech recognition software. While speech recognition was much faster than using the on-screen keyboard, however, it was still not fast enough for James to complete all of his work within the allotted time. Therefore, he took a reduced course load and aimed at finishing his degree in 5 to 6 years, instead of the typical 4-year period.*

### Questions

1. What would be involved in planning for James's changing needs?

2. How far ahead would you plan? Why?

3. Who needs to be involved in the planning?

4. What other AT would be of benefit to James?

Isabel Killoran is an Associate Professor at the Faculty of Education, York University, Toronto, Canada. She is also associated with the graduate programme in Critical Disability Studies at York. Some of the courses she has taught include inclusion at the primary/junior level, curriculum study, human development and socialization, and educating young children. She is an active member of many national and international professional organizations and was the president of the Ontario subdivision of the Division for Early Childhood of the Council for Exceptional Children (DEC). Her interest in inclusion stems from the resistance and frustration she experienced trying to get special education students included while she was a special education and classroom teacher. Her current focus is on preservice and practicing teachers understanding the importance of inclusion and their role in making it a reality. Other research areas include teacher attitudes, preschool/primary inclusion, and adults with intellectual disabilities working as self-advocates.

Mark Brown is currently an Assistant Professor at Daeman College in Amherst, New York, where he teaches special education and education classes to both undergraduate and graduate students. His research interest pertains to identifying best "inclusionary practices" for children with special needs in early childhood preschool settings. Prior to pursuing his doctoral degree, he was a special education teacher in the Buffalo public school system. He instructed students, ages 10-12, in a cross-categorical special education classroom for three years. Brown is a member of the national Council of Exceptional Children, the New York State Council for Exceptional Children, the Division for Early Childhood, and the Association for Childhood Education International.

Nancy Adams is an elementary school teacher with the Durham District School Board in Ontario, Canada. She has enjoyed teaching students at the grades 3 through 5 level, both within an integrated and an inclusive public school setting, over the past seven years. While working in an urban community, Nancy has implemented inclusive teaching practices to meet the diverse needs of the learners (students with learning differences who have an Individualized Education Plan, students with cultural and racial differences, and those learning English as a Second Language) in her classroom and throughout the school. As a master of education graduate from York University with an avid interest in anti-bias education, Adams has researched the impact of province-wide testing on students at the grade 3 level and parents' perceptions of this criterion-referenced test. Currently, she is pursuing a doctorate degree in education at the Ontario Institute for Studies in Education from the University of Toronto with a focus on Curriculum Studies.

Billie L. Friedland is an Associate Professor of Special Education Teacher Preparation at Delaware State University in Dover. She serves as Education Department Curriculum Committee Chair, Hearing Master for DSU Judicial Affairs Committee, Mentorship Coordinator for STEP Scholars, and Faculty Sponsor for the Student Chapter of the Council for Exceptional Children. Friedland's work is published in *Special Education Leadership Review*, *Rural Special Education Quarterly*, and *ACRES Conference Proceedings*. She is an active member of the American Association on Mental Retardation, the American Council on Rural Special Education, Council for Exception Children, and the National Educational Fraternity, Phi Delta Kappa. She is a long-time member of NAACP, and is a past Western Regional Recording Secretary of the Conference on Black Basic Education. She also has 17 years of experience in community agency services to people with mental retardation.

Patricia F. Hearron is a Professor of Child Development and Coordinator of the Birth-through-Kindergarten teacher preparation program at Appalachian State University in Boone, North Carolina. In addition to more than 20 years' experience teaching graduate and undergraduate courses in early childhood education, she has taught young children in the United States, China, and Rwanda; directed child development programs; and served as a licensing consultant. She is co-author (with Verna Hildebrand) of two textbooks: *Management of Child Development Programs* and *Guiding Young Children*. Her particular interest is the early childhood programs of Reggio Emilia, Italy, and inclusion of children with special rights.

Jennifer Horgan resides in Miami Township outside of Cincinnati, Ohio. She earned her B.S.Ed. in early childhood education from the University of Cincinnati in June of 2006. Horgan completed her teaching experiences at Arlitt Child & Family Research & Education Center, Fairfield Kindergarten Center, and Sayler Park Elementary. Literacy development and differentiating instruction to motivate and meet the needs of all ability levels are her two main interests within education. During her undergraduate career, Horgan was recognized by the University of Cincinnati for exemplifying *high moral and academic standards of a primary teacher—who is sensitive, loving and understanding of little children*, a requirement of the prestigious Pearl M. Wright Award established to support the training of future teachers. She strives to live up to these high standards and is looking forward to the adventures ahead.

Neita Israelite is Associate Professor in the Faculty of Education at York University in Toronto, Ontario. She teaches courses related to disability issues in the Faculties of Education and Arts, as well as the Graduate Program in Critical Disability Studies. In addition, she works in York's Teacher Preparation Program in the Education of Deaf and Hard of Hearing Students. She received her master's and doctoral degrees from the University of Pittsburgh. Her research focuses on secondary and postsecondary experiences of students with disabilities.

Mike Malone, Professor of Early Childhood Education and Coordinator of the Early Childhood Intervention Special Program at the University of Cincinnati, currently resides in Oxford, Ohio. Malone received his B.A. in Psychology from the University of Cincinnati and his M.S. and Ph.D. from The University of Georgia. He has an extensive background in early childhood intervention, interdisciplinary program development, personnel preparation, and research. His specific areas of focus include children's play in school and family contexts, early transitions, higher education personnel preparation and program development, team processes, and observational methodology. He has directed and served on numerous federal and state grants designed to promote systems change through professional development and has developed and taught a number of courses in early childhood intervention (e.g., foundations, contexts, families, teams, inclusive environments, play, and observation and assessment techniques). Finally, Malone has published and presented numerous works on issues related to early childhood intervention.

Sonia Mastrangelo is currently completing her Ph.D. at York University in education, with a focus on parents with children who have autism spectrum disorder. She is working as a research assistant with the Milton and Ethel Harris Research Initiative in the department of psychology, acquiring experience in conducting clinical assessments with parents. She has been a special educator for nine years, both in contained and inclusive environments, for the Dufferin Peel Catholic District School Board. She completed her M.A. at the Ontario Institute for Studies in Education/University of Toronto in 2001. Mastrangelo currently holds an Ontario Graduate Scholarship and will be teaching her first inclusion course at York University next term.

Jennifer Mays is a registered occupational therapist as well as a certified teacher. She has received both bachelor of science and bachelor of education degrees. Mays has worked as an OT at Bloorview Kids Rehab for over four years in the field of augmentative and alternative communication. She has been involved in research on the experience of developing typing skills and on the effectiveness of word cueing technology.

Angela Pitamber currently teaches high school English at Harold M. Brathwaite Secondary School, in Brampton, Ontario. She graduated from York University with a double major in political science and English, and also worked on her bachelor of education and master's of education at York University. Being an immigrant to Canada, she has an awareness of the necessity for accommodations to different needs and types of learners. Teaching in a secondary setting allows her to work with students with various learning disabilities, and to address the challenge of findings ways in which to best facilitate their learning.

Kim Roth currently resides in Cincinnati, Ohio. She earned her B.S.Ed. in early childhood education from the University of Cincinnati in 2005 and works as an Intervention Specialist for children with moderate to severe disabilities. Roth's expertise lies in early childhood education and inclusion with particular interest in trends in education and how the needs of all children can be better met throughout education. She received the Most Outstanding Student Award upon graduating with her B.S.Ed., and served as President of UC Chapter of the Student Council for Exceptional Children and the Vice President of Kappa Delta Pi.

Lucia Schroeder is an Assistant Professor of Early Childhood, Elementary and Middle Level Education at Eastern Illinois University. She has been a teacher in inclusive K-12 education settings, including Title One; elementary education, grades 1-6; and junior-senior high vocational family and consumer science. She has taught at the university level for 5 years, with an emphasis in literacy education. Schroeder also has presented at state and regional reading conferences.

Karen Swartz has been the Manager of the Office for Persons with Disabilities at York University since 1988. She has a master's degree in social work from York University, and she is currently a doctoral candidate in York's Graduate Program in Language, Culture and Teaching. In 2001, she was the recipient of an Ontario Ministry of Citizenship, Community Action Award. Swartz's research focuses on postsecondary transitions for students with disabilities.

Cynthia Tam received her master of science degree from the University of Toronto, Canada. She is the Professional Practice Leader for Occupational Therapy at Bloorview Kids Rehab in Toronto. She is also an Assistant Professor with the Department of Occupational Science and Occupational Therapy, Faculty of Medicine, University of Toronto. She has over 20 years of experience working in the field of assistive technology for adults and children. Tam has been involved in the development of adaptive computer software, such as WiViK and WordQ. As a clinician investigator with the Bloorview Research Institute, she has been awarded research grants for projects related to handwriting, development of assistive technology, and evaluation of outcomes of technology intervention.

Gail Teachman is completing her master of science degree at the Graduate Department of Rehabilitation Science, Faculty of Medicine, University of Toronto. She is also a Lecturer with the Department of Occupational Science and Occupational Therapy at the same university. She currently works at Bloorview Kids Rehab in Toronto, Canada. She has over 20 years of experience working with children in Canada and in the United States, primarily as a consultant to schools. Teachman has been honored with two teaching awards: one from University of Toronto, Faculty of Medicine, and one from University of Manitoba, School of Medical Rehabilitation. She has been awarded research grants for projects related to intervention and outcome measurement in the field of augmentative and alternative communication.

Lynn Walz has worked for more than 20 years in the field of special education. She has been a champion of inclusive learning environments for all learners. Walz has many years of experience in high schools as a case manager of students with disabilities, teaching basic skills and consulting with content area teachers to design accommodations for the classroom. In addition, Walz has participated in several research and training projects related to inclusive education and full participation of students with disabilities in the general curriculum. Walz was a project coordinator for Together We're Better and a research assistant for National Center for Educational Outcomes. As well as teaching teens with disabilities, Walz has provided training for educators through a variety of workshops and college courses, many specifically focused on accommodating all learners in the classroom.